TEACHER CERTIFICATION EXAM

TExES™
GENERAL SCIENCE
MIDDLE SCHOOL

Written by:

Kelly Benson, BS Earth Science
Jenny Ellis, BS Chemistry
Lynn Slygh, MS Biology
Sharon Wynne, BS General Science

Edited By:
Patricia Wynne, BS Microbiology

To order additional copies:
Xamonline, Inc.
21 Orient Avenue
Melrose, MA 02176

Phone: 1-800-301-4647
Email: winwin1111@aol.com
Web: www.xamonline.com
Fax: 1-781-662-9268
Toll free: 1-800-301-4647

You will find:

- Content review in prose format
- Sample test
- Answers with explanations

XAMonline, INC.
Building Better Teachers

"And, while there's no reason yet to panic, I think it's only prudent that we make preparations to panic."

GENERAL SCIENCE
TExES™ ISBN: 1-58197-108-7

COMPETENCY 1.0   KNOWLEDGE OF SCIENTIFIC PROCESSES AND THE LABORATORY.

SKILL 1.1   Apply knowledge of the primary processes of science: observing, inferring, measuring (metric system), communicating/graphing, and classifying.

Science may be defined as a body of knowledge that is systematically derived from study, observations and experimentation. Its goal is to identify and establish principles and theories which may be applied to solve problems. Pseudoscience, on the other hand, is a belief that is not warranted. There is no scientific methodology or application. Some of the more classic examples of pseudoscience include witchcraft, alien encounters, or any topics that are explained by hearsay.

Science uses the metric system as it is accepted worldwide and allows easier comparison among experiments done by scientists around the world. Learn the following basic units and prefixes:

meter - measure of length
liter - measure of volume
gram - measure of mass

deca-(meter, liter, gram)= 10X the base unit   **deci** = 1/10 the base unit
hecto-(meter, liter, gram)= 100X the base unit   **centi** = 1/100 the base unit
kilo-(meter, liter, gram) = 1000X the base unit   **milli** = 1/1000 the base unit

Graphing is an important skill to visually display collected data for analysis. The two types of graphs most commonly used are the **line graph** and the **bar graph** (histogram). Line graphs are set up to show two variables represented by one point on the graph. The X axis is the horizontal axis and represents the dependent variable. Dependent variables are those that would be present independently of the experiment. A common example of a dependent variable is time. Time proceeds regardless of anything else going on. The Y axis is the vertical axis and represents the independent variable. Independent variables are manipulated by the experiment, such as the amount of light, or the height of a plant. Graphs should be calibrated at equal intervals. If one space represents one day, the next space may not represent ten days. A "best fit" line is drawn to join the points and may not include all the points in the data. Axes must always be labeled, or the graph means nothing. A good title will describe both the dependent and the independent variable. Bar graphs are set up similarly in regards to axes, but points are not plotted. Instead, the dependent variable is set up as a bar where the X axis intersects with the Y axis. Each bar is a separate item of data and is not joined by a continuous line.

Classifying is grouping items according to their similarities. It is important for students to realize relationships and similarity as well as differences to reach a reasonable conclusion in a lab experience.

SKILL 1.2   Apply knowledge of the integrated processes of science: forming hypothesis, manipulating variables (manipulated, responding, held constant), defining operationally, interpreting data, and using indirect evidence and models.

The scientific method is the basic process behind science. It involves several steps from formulating a hypothesis to the conclusion.

Posing a question
Although many discoveries happen by chance the standard thought process of a scientist begins with forming a question to research. The more limited the question, the easier it is to set up an experiment to answer it.

Form a hypothesis.
Once the question is formulated take an educated guess about the answer to the problem or question.

Doing the test
To make a test fair data from an experiment must have a **variable** or any condition that can be changed such as temperature or mass. A good test will try to manipulate as few variables as possible so as to see which variable is responsible for the result. This requires a second example of a **control**. A control is an extra setup in which all the conditions are the same except for the variable being tested.

Observe and record the data
Reporting of the data should state specifics of how the measurements were calculated. A graduated cylinder needs to be read with proper procedures. As beginning students, technique must be part of the instructional process so as to give validity to the data.

Drawing a conclusion
After you take your data you compare it with that from the other groups. A conclusion is the judgment derived from the data results.

Graphing data
Graphing takes numbers and demonstrates patterns that might otherwise be harder to make conclusions from.

SKILL 1.3   Apply knowledge of designing and performing investigations.

Normally, knowledge is integrated in the form of a lab report. It should include a specific title and tell exactly what is being studied. The abstract is a summary of the report written at the beginning of the paper. The purpose should always be defined and will state the problem. The purpose should include the **hypothesis** (educated guess) of what is expected from the outcome of the experiment. The entire experiment should relate to this problem. It is important to describe exactly what was done to prove or disprove a hypothesis. A **control** is necessary to prove that the results occurred from the changed conditions and would not just happen normally. Only one variable should be manipulated at one time. **Observations** and results of the experiment should be recorded including all results from data. Drawings, graphs and illustrations should be included to support information. Observations are objective, whereas analysis and interpretation is subjective. A **conclusion** should explain why the results of the experiment either proved or disproved the hypothesis.

A scientific theory is an explanation of a set of related observations based on a proven hypothesis. A scientific law usually lasts longer than a scientific theory and has more data to back it up.

SKILL 1.4   Perform basic science calculations (e.g. molar, percent solutions, proportions and rates).

Moles = mass X 1 mole/molecular weight

For example, to determine the moles of 20 grams of water, you would take the mass of the water (20 g) and multiply it by 1 mole of water divided by the molecular weight of a molecule of water (18 g).

Percent solution and **proportions** are basically the same thing. To find percent volume, divide the grams of the substance by the amount of the solvent. For example, 20 grams of salt divided by 100 ml of water would result in a 20% solution of saltwater. To determine percent mass, divide the ml of substance being mixed by the amount of solvent. Percent mass is not used as often as percent volume.

Rate is determined by dividing the change in distance (or the independent variable) by the change in time. If a plant grew four inches in two days, the rate of growth would be two inches per day.

SKILL 1.5   Identify procedures for proper use, care and handling of laboratory animals, plants and protists.

Dissections - Animals which are not obtained from recognized sources should not be used. Decaying animals or those of unknown origin may harbor pathogens and/or parasites. Specimens should be rinsed before handling. Latex gloves are desirable. If gloves are not available, students with sores or scratches should be excused from the activity. Formaldehyde is a carcinogenic and should be avoided or disposed of according to district regulations. Students objecting to dissections for moral reasons should be given an alternative assignment.

Live specimens - No dissections may be performed on living mammalian vertebrates or birds. Lower order life and invertebrates may be used. Biological experiments may be done with all animals except mammalian vertebrates or birds. No physiological harm may result to the animal. All animals housed and cared for in the school must be handled in a safe and humane manner. Animals are not to remain on school premises during extended vacations unless adequate care is provided. Many state laws state that any instructor who intentionally refuses to comply with the laws may be suspended or dismissed.

Microbiology - Pathogenic organisms must never be used for experimentation. Students should adhere to the following rules at all times when working with microorganisms to avoid accidental contamination:

1. Treat all microorganisms as if they were pathogenic.
2. Maintain sterile conditions at all times

If you are taking a national level exam you should check the Department of Education for your state for safety procedures. You will want to know what your state expects of you not only for the test but also for performance in the classroom for the good welfare of your students and others.

SKILL 1.6   Identify the laboratory equipment to be used for specified activities (e.g. voltmeter, volumetric flask, hygrometer, microscope and balance).

Bunsen burners - Hot plates should be used whenever possible to avoid the risk of burns or fire. If Bunsen burners are used, the following precautions should be followed:

1. Know the location of fire extinguishers and safety blankets and train students in their use. Long hair and long sleeves should be secured and out of the way.

2. Turn the gas all the way on and make a spark with the striker.

3. Adjust the air valve at the bottom of the Bunsen burner until the flame shows an inner cone.

4. Adjust the flow of gas to the desired flame height by using the adjustment valve.

5. Do not touch the barrel of the burner as it is hot.

6. The preferred method to light burners is to use strikers rather than matches.

Graduated Cylinder - These are used for precise measurements. They should always be placed on a flat surface. The surface of the liquid will form a meniscus (a lens-shaped curve). The measurement is read at the bottom of this curve.

Balance - Electronic balances are easier to use, but more expensive. An electronic balance should always be tarred before measuring and used on a flat surface. Substances should always be placed on a piece of paper to avoid messes and damage to the instrument. Triple beam balances must be used on a level surface. There are screws located at the bottom of the balance to make any adjustments. Start with the largest counterweight first to the last notch that does not tip the balance. Do the same with the next largest, etc until the pointer remains at zero. The total mass is the total of all the readings on the beams. Again, use paper under the substance to protect the equipment.

Buret – A buret is used to dispense precisely measured volumes of liquid. A stopcock is used to control the volume of liquid being dispensed at a time.

Light microscopes are commonly used in laboratory experiments. Several procedures should be followed to properly care for this equipment:

- Clean all lenses with lens paper only.
- Carry microscopes with two hands; one on the arm and one on the base.
- Always begin focusing on low power, then switch to high power.
- Store microscopes with the low power objective down.
- Always use a coverslip when viewing wet mount slides.
- Bring the objective down to its lowest position then focus moving up to avoid breaking the slide or scratching the lens.

Wet mount slides should be made by placing a drop of water on the specimen and then putting a glass coverslip on top of the drop of water. Dropping the coverslip at a forty-five degree angle will help in avoiding air bubbles
Total magnification is determined by multiplying the ocular (usually 10X) and the objective (usually 10X on low, 40X on high).

SKILL 1.7   Identify sources of laboratory materials and adequate substitutions.

Lab materials are readily available from the many school suppliers that routinely send their catalogues to schools. Many times, common materials are available at the local grocery store. The use of locally available flora and fauna both reduces the cost and familiarizes students with the organisms where they live. Innovation and networking with other science teachers will assist in keeping costs of lab materials to a minimum.

SKILL 1.8   Identify state laws or regulations related to teaching science.

All science labs should contain the following items of safety equipment. The following are requirements by law.

- Fire blanket which is visible and accessible
- Ground Fault Circuit Interrupters (GCFI) within two feet of water supplies signs designating room exits
- Emergency shower providing a continuous flow of water
- Emergency eye wash station which can be activated by the foot or forearm
- Eye protection for every student and a means of sanitizing equipment
- Emergency exhaust fans providing ventilation to the outside of the building
- Master cut-off switches for gas, electric and compressed air. Switches must have permanently attached handles. Cut-off switches must be clearly labeled.
- An ABC fire extinguisher
- Storage cabinets for flammable materials

Also recommended, but not required by law:
- Chemical spill control kit
- Fume hood with a motor which is spark proof
- Protective laboratory aprons made of flame retardant material
- Signs which will alert potential hazardous conditions
- Containers for broken glassware, flammables, corrosives and waste.
- Containers should be labeled.

It is the responsibility of teachers to provide a safe environment for their students. Proper supervision greatly reduces the risk of injury and a teacher should never leave a class for any reason without providing alternate supervision. After an accident, two factors are considered; foreseeability and negligence. **Foreseeability** is the anticipation that an event may occur under certain circumstances. **Negligence** is the failure to exercise ordinary or reasonable care. Safety procedures should be a part of the science curriculum and a well managed classroom is important to avoid potential lawsuits

The **"Right to Know Law" statutes** cover science teachers who work with potentially hazardous chemicals. Briefly, the law states that employees must be informed of potentially toxic chemicals. An inventory must be made available if requested. The inventory must contain information about the hazards and properties of the chemicals. Training must be provided in the safe handling and interpretation of the Material Safety Data Sheet.

GENERAL SCIENCE

The following chemicals are potential carcinogens and not allowed in school facilities:

Acrylonitriel, Arsenic compounds, Asbestos, Bensidine, Benzene, Cadmium compounds, Chloroform, Chromium compounds, Ethylene oxide, Ortho-toluidine, Nickle powder, Mercury.

SKILL 1.9   Identify the accepted procedures for safe use, storage, and disposal of chemicals.

All laboratory solutions should be prepared as directed in the lab manual. Care should be taken to avoid contamination. All glassware should be rinsed thoroughly with distilled water before using, and cleaned well after use. Safety goggles should be worn while working with glassware in case of an accident. All solutions should be made with distilled water as tap water contains dissolved particles which may affect the results of an experiment. Chemical storage should be located in a secured, dry area. Chemicals should be stored in accordance with reactability. Acids are to be locked in a separate area. Used solutions should be disposed of according to local disposal procedures. Any questions regarding safe disposal or chemical safety may be directed to the local fire department.

SKILL 1.10 Identify current technology and its uses in the sciences (e.g. computerization, satellites, sonar, seismographic instrumentation, medicine, agriculture and spectrometry).

Chromatography uses the principles of capillarity to separate substances such as plant pigments. Molecules of a larger size will move slower up the paper, whereas smaller molecules will move more quickly producing lines of pigments.

Spectrophotometry uses percent light absorbance to measure a color change, thus giving qualitative data a quantitative value.

Centrifugation involves spinning substances at a high speed. The more dense part of a solution will settle to the bottom of the test tube, where the lighter material will stay on top. Centrifugation is used to separate blood into blood cells and plasma, with the heavier blood cells settling to the bottom.

Electrophoresis uses electrical charges of molecules to separate them according to their size. The molecules, such as DNA or proteins are pulled through a gel towards either the positive end of the gel box (if the material has a negative charge) or the negative end of the gel box (if the material has a positive charge).

Computer technology has greatly improved the collection and interpretation of scientific data. Molecular findings have been enhanced through the use of computer images. Technology has revolutionized the access to data via the internet and shared databases. The manipulation of the data has much more sophisticated software capabilities. The computer engineering advances have produced such products as MRIs and CT scans in medicine and laser technology with numerous applications refining precision.

Satellites have improved our ability to communicate and transmit radio and television signals. Navigational abilities have been greatly improved through the use of satellite signals. Sonar uses sound waves to locate objects, especially underwater. The sound waves bounce off the object and are picked up to assist in location. Seismographs record vibrations in the earth and allow us to measure earthquake activity.

GENERAL SCIENCE

COMPETENCY 2.0 KNOWLEDGE OF CHEMISTRY

SKILL 2.1   Identify the physical and chemical properties of matter (e.g. mass, weight, volume, identity, and reactivity).

Everything in our world is made up of **matter**, whether it is a rock, a building, an animal, or a person. Matter is defined by its characteristics: It takes up space and it has mass.

Mass is a measure of the amount of matter in an object. Two objects of equal mass will balance each other on a simple balance scale no matter where the scale is located. For instance, two rocks with the same amount of mass that are in balance on earth will also be in balance on the moon. They will feel heavier on earth than on the moon because of the gravitational pull of the earth. So, although the two rocks have the same mass, they will have different **weight.**

Weight is the measure of the earth's pull of gravity on an object. It can also be defined as the pull of gravity between other bodies. The units of weight measure that we commonly use are the pound in English measure and the kilogram in metric measure.

In addition to mass, matter also has the property of volume. **Volume** is the amount of cubic space that an object occupies. Volume and mass together give a more exact description of the object. Two objects may have the same volume, but different mass, the same mass but different volumes, etc. For instance, consider two cubes that are each one cubic centimeter, one made from plastic, one from lead. They have the same volume, but the lead cube has more mass. The measure that we use to describe the cubes takes into consideration both the mass and the volume. **Density** is the mass of a substance contained per unit of volume. If the density of an object is less than the density of a liquid, the object will float in the liquid. If the object is denser than the liquid, then the object will sink.

Density is stated in grams per cubic centimeter (g / cm^3) where the gram is the standard unit of mass. To find an object's density, you must measure its mass and its volume. Then divide the mass by the volume ($D = m / V$).

To find an object's density, first use a balance to find its mass. Then calculate its volume. If the object is a regular shape, you can find the volume by multiplying the length, width, and height together. However, if it is an irregular shape, you can find the volume by seeing how much water it displaces. Measure the water in the container before and after the object is submerged. The difference will be the volume of the object.

Specific gravity is the ratio of the density of a substance to the density of water. For instance, the specific density of one liter of turpentine is calculated by comparing its mass (0.81 kg) to the mass of one liter of water (1 kg):

$$\frac{\text{mass of 1 L alcohol}}{\text{mass of 1 L water}} = \frac{0.81 \text{ kg}}{1.00 \text{ kg}} = 0.81$$

Physical properties and chemical properties of matter describe the appearance or behavior of a substance. A **physical property** can be observed without changing the identity of a substance. For instance, you can describe the color, mass, shape, and volume of a book. **Chemical properties** describe the ability of a substance to be changed into new substances. Baking powder goes through a chemical change as it changes into carbon dioxide gas during the baking process.

Matter constantly changes. A **physical change** is a change that does not produce a new substance. The freezing and melting of water is an example of physical change. A **chemical change (or chemical reaction)** is any change of a substance into one or more other substances. Burning materials turn into smoke, a seltzer tablet fizzes into gas bubbles.

SKILL 2.2   Distinguish among solids, liquids, and gases.

The **phase of matter** (solid, liquid, or gas) is identified by its shape and volume. A **solid** has a definite shape and volume. A **liquid** has a definite volume, but no shape. A **gas** has no shape or volume because it will spread out to occupy the entire space of whatever container it is in.

Energy is the ability to cause change in matter. Applying heat to a frozen liquid changes it from solid back to liquid. Continue heating it and it will boil and give off steam, a gas.

Evaporation is the change in phase from liquid to gas. **Condensation** is the change in phase from gas to liquid.

SKILL 2.3   Apply knowledge of the gas laws (e.g. relationships among temperature, pressure, and volume of gases).

As a substance is heated, the molecules begin moving faster within the container. As the substance becomes a gas and those molecules hit the sides of the container, pressure builds. **Pressure** is the force exerted on each unit of area of a surface. Pressure is measured in a unit called the **Pascal**. One Pascal (pa) is equal to one Newton of force pushing on one square meter of area.

Volume, temperature, and pressure of gas are related.

Temperature and pressure: As the temperature of a gas increases, its pressure increases. When you drive a car, the friction between the road and the tire heats up the air inside the tire. Because the temperature increases, so does the pressure of the air on the inside of the tire.

Temperature and Volume: at a constant pressure, an increase in temperature causes an increase in the volume of a gas. If you apply heat to an enclosed container of gas, the pressure inside the bottle will increase as the heat increases. This is called **Charles' Law**.

These relations (pressure and temperature, and temperature and volume) are **direct variations**. As one component increases (decreases), the other also increases (decreases).

However, pressure and volume vary inversely.

Pressure and volume: At a constant temperature, a decrease in the volume of a gas causes an increase in its pressure. An example of this is a tire pump. The gas pressure inside the pump gets bigger as you press down on the pump handle because you are compressing the gas, or forcing it to exist in a smaller volume. This relationship between pressure and volume is called **Boyle's Law**.

SKILL 2.4   Identify the characteristics of elements, compounds, and mixtures.

An **element** is a substance that can not be broken down into other substances. Today, scientists have identified 109 elements: 89 are found in nature and 20 are synthetic.

An **atom** is the smallest particle of the element that has the properties of that element. All of the atoms of a particular element are the same. The atoms of each element are different from the atoms of the other elements.

Elements are assigned an identifying symbol of one or two letters. The symbol for oxygen is O and stands for one atom of oxygen. However, because oxygen atoms in nature are joined together is pairs, the symbol O_2 represents oxygen. This pair of oxygen molecules is a molecule. A **molecule** is the smallest particle of substance that can exist independently and has all of the properties of that substance. A molecule of most elements is made up of one atom. However, oxygen, hydrogen, nitrogen, and chlorine molecules are made of two atoms each.

A **compound** is made of two or more elements that have been chemically combined. Atoms join together when elements are chemically combined. The result is that the elements lose their individual identities when they are joined. The compound that they become has different properties.

We use a formula to show the elements of a chemical compound. A **chemical formula** is a shorthand way of showing what is in a compound by using symbols and subscripts. The letter symbols let us know what elements are involved and the number subscript tells how many atoms of each element are involved. No subscript is used if there is only one atom involved. For example, carbon dioxide is made up of one atom of carbon (C) and two atoms of oxygen (O_2), so the formula would be represented as: CO_2.

Substances can combine without a chemical change. A **mixture** is any combination of two or more substances in which the substances keep their own properties. A fruit salad is a mixture. So is an ice cream sundae, although you might not recognize each part if it is stirred together. Colognes and perfumes are the other examples. You may not readily recognize the individual elements. However, they can be separated.

Compounds and **mixtures** are similar in that they are made up of two or more substances. However, they have the following opposite characteristics:

Compounds:
1. Made up of one kind of particle
2. Formed during a chemical change
3. Broken down only by chemical changes
4. Properties are different from its parts
5. Has a specific amount of each ingredient.

Mixtures:
1. Made up of two or more particles
2. Not formed by a chemical change
3. Can be separated by physical changes
4. Properties are the same as its parts.
5. Does not have a definite amount of each ingredient.

Common compounds are **acid, base, salt,** and **oxides** and are classified according to their characteristics.

An **acid** contains one element of hydrogen (H). Although it is never wise to taste a substance to identify it, acids have a sour taste. Vinegar and lemon juice are both acids, and acids occur in many foods in a weak state. Strong acids can burn skin and destroy materials. Common acids include:

Sulfuric acid (H_2SO_4)	-	Used in medicines, alcohol, dyes, and car batteries.
Nitric acid (HNO_3)	-	Used in fertilizers, explosives, cleaning materials.
Carbonic acid (H_2CO_3)	-	Used in soft drinks.
Acetic acid ($HC_2H_3O_2$)	-	Used in making plastics, rubber, photographic film, and as a solvent.

Bases have a bitter taste and the stronger ones feel slippery. Like acids, strong bases can be dangerous and should be handled carefully. All bases contain the elements oxygen and hydrogen (OH). Many household cleaning products contain bases. Common bases include:

Sodium hydroxide	NaOH	-	Used in making soap, paper, vegetable oils, and refining petroleum.
Ammonium hydroxide	NH_4OH	-	Making deodorants, bleaching compounds, cleaning compounds.
Potassium hydroxide	KOH	-	Making soaps, drugs, dyes, alkaline batteries, and purifying industrial gases.
Calcium hydroxide	$Ca(OH)_2$	-	Making cement and plaster

An **indicator** is a substance that changes color when it comes in contact with an acid or a base. Litmus paper is an indicator. Blue litmus paper turns red in an acid. Red litmus paper turns blue in a base.

A substance that is neither acid nor base is **neutral**. Neutral substances do not change the color of litmus paper.

Salt is formed when an acid and a base combine chemically. Water is also formed. The process is called **neutralization**. Table salt (NaCl) is an example of this process. Salts are also used in toothpaste, epsom salts, and cream of tartar. Calcium chloride ($CaCl_2$) is used on frozen streets and walkways to melt the ice.

Oxides are compounds that are formed when oxygen combines with another element. Rust is an oxide formed when oxygen combines with iron.

SKILL 2.5 Apply knowledge of symbols, formulas, and equations related to common elements and compounds and their reactions.

One or more substances are formed during a **chemical reaction**. Also, energy is released during some chemical reactions. Sometimes the energy release is slow and sometimes it is rapid. In a fireworks display, energy is released very rapidly. However, the chemical reaction that produces tarnish on a silver spoon happens very slowly.

Chemical equilibrium is defined as when the quantities of reactants and products are at a 'steady state' and no longer shifting, but the reaction may still proceed forward and backward. The rate of forward reaction must equal the rate of backward reaction.

For more information on chemical reactions, also see section 2.11: Identify types of chemical reactions and their characteristics.

In one kind of chemical reaction, two elements combine to form a new substance. We can represent the reaction and the results in a chemical equation.

Carbon and oxygen form carbon dioxide. The equation can be written:

$$C \quad + \quad O_2 \quad \rightarrow \quad CO_2$$

| 1 atom of | + | 1 atom of | $\rightarrow$ | 1 molecule of |
| carbon | | oxygen | $\rightarrow$ | carbon dioxide |

No matter is ever gained or lost during a chemical reaction; therefore the chemical equation must be *balanced*. This means that there must be the same number of molecules on both sides of the equation. Remember that the subscript numbers indicate the number of atoms in the elements. If there is no subscript, assume there is only one atom.

In a second kind of chemical reaction, the molecules of a substance split forming two or more new substances. An electric current can split water molecules into hydrogen and oxygen gas.

$$2H_2O \quad \rightarrow \quad 2H_2 \quad - \quad O_2$$

| 2 molecules | $\rightarrow$ | 2 molecules | - | 1 molecule |
| of water | | of hydrogen | | of oxygen |

The number of molecules is shown by the number in front of an element or compound. If no number appears, assume that it is 1 molecule.

A third kind of chemical reaction is when elements change places with each other. An example of one element taking the place of another is when iron changes places with copper in the compound copper sulfate:

$CuSo_4$	+	Fe	$\rightarrow$	$FeSO_4$+	Cu
copper sulfate	+	iron (steel wool)		iron sulfate	copper

Sometimes two sets of elements change places. In this example, an acid and a base are combined:

HCl	+	NaOH	$\rightarrow$	NaCl	+	H_2O
hydrochloric acid		sodium hydroxide		sodium chloride (table salt)		water

Matter can change, but it can not be created nor destroyed. The sample equations show two things:

1. In a chemical reaction, matter is changed into one or more different kinds of matter.
2. The amount of matter present before and after the chemical reaction is the same.

Many chemical reactions give off energy. Like matter, energy can change form but it can neither be created nor destroyed during a chemical reaction. This is the **law of conservation of energy.**

SKILL 2.6   Identify the major events in the development of the atomic theory.

The **atomic theory of matter** suggests that:

1. All matter consists of atoms
2. All atoms of an element are identical
3. Different elements have different atoms
4. Atoms maintain their properties in a chemical reaction

The atomic theory of matter was first suggested by a Greek named **Democritus.** The atomic theory of matter states that matter is made up of tiny, rapidly moving particles. These particles move more quickly when warmer, because temperature is a measure of average kinetic energy of the particles. Warmer molecules therefore move further away from each other, with enough energy to separate from each other more often and for greater distances.

Much later (1780's), a scientist named **John Dalton** expanded on Democritus' idea. Dalton, a school teacher, made some observations about air: air is a mixture of different kinds of gases; these gases do not separate on their own; it is possible to compress gases into a smaller volume. He also thought that particles of different substances must be different from each other and must maintain their own mass when combined with other substances.

Dalton's Model of the Atom:

1. Matter is made up of atoms.
2. Atoms of an element are similar to each other.
3. Atoms of different elements are different from each other.
4. Atoms combine with each other to form new kinds of compounds.

The present model of the atom is much different from Dalton's model.

In the late 1800's, a British scientist named **Thompson** was studying how electric current flowed through a vacuum tube. His hypothesis was:

1. If rays are made of charged particles, then an electric field would attract them.
2. If it is a charged particle, then a magnet will affect its motion.

From his work, Thompson proved that the rays were made of negative particles. These particles were later called electrons.

The results of his experimentation produced **Thompson's Model:** The atom is made of negative particles equally mixed in a sphere of positive material.

In 1986 it was discovered that some elements give off particles with a positive charge. These elements have 7,000 times the mass of electrons. The British scientist **Ernest Rutherford** called these **alpha particles**. He used the alpha particles to test Thompson's model. He hammered gold foil until it was less than 1mm thick and then fired alpha particles at the foil. He used a telescope and a screen to locate the alpha particles. His hypothesis was that if Thompson's theory was right, then the alpha particles would pass through the foil in a straight line. He found that most particles passed through as expected. However, some appeared to bounce off in another direction. This could not be explained by Thompson's model. The result of his experiment gave way to **Rutherford's Model**:

1. Most of the atom is empty space. (This explains why most of the alpha particles pass directly through it).
2. The center of the atom contains a nucleus containing most of the mass and all of the positively charge of the atom.
3. The scattering of particles is occurs when they collide with the nucleus.
4. The region of the space outside the nucleus is occupied by electrons.
5. The atom is neutral because the protons in the nucleus equal the electrons in the space outside the nucleus.

Based on Rutherford's model, scientists thought that the electrons of an atom might orbit the nucleus much like the planets orbit the sun. If this is true, they could expect two things:

1. As electrons orbit, they give off light energy continuously. If this light energy is passed through a prism, it would produce a band of color.
2. As the orbiting electrons gave off light, they would lose energy and spiral into the nucleus of the atom causing the atom to collapse. Therefore, the atom would take up no space.

No color band was observed. Instead, lines of color and dark lines were observed. Also, since we know that because matter does in fact take up space, then the orbiting atoms can not collapse into nothing. Another model was necessary to explain the observations. The Danish scientist **Neils Bohr** created a model in 1913. The results of his model are:

1. Electrons orbit the nucleus, but only certain orbits are allowed. An electron in an allowed orbit will not lose energy.
2. When an electron moves from an outer orbit to an inner orbit, it gives off energy.
3. When an electron moves from an inner orbit to an outer orbit, it absorbs energy.

Bohr's model only explains the very simplest atoms, such as hydrogen. Today's more sophisticated atomic model is based upon how waves react.

SKILL 2.7   Identify the major components of the atom and their characteristics and functions.

An **atom** is a nucleus surrounded by a cloud with moving electrons.

The **nucleus** is the center of the atom. The positive particles inside the nucleus are called **protons.** The mass of a proton is about 2,000 times that of the mass of an electron. The number of protons in the nucleus of an atom is called the **atomic number.** All atoms of the same element have the same atomic number.

Neutrons are another type of particle in the nucleus. Neutrons and protons have about the same mass, but neutrons have no charge. Neutrons were discovered because scientists observed that not all atoms in neon gas have the same mass. They had identified isotopes. **Isotopes** of an element have the same number of protons in the nucleus, but have different masses. Neutrons explain the difference in mass. They have mass but no charge.

The mass of matter is measured against a standard mass such as the gram. Scientists measure the mass of an atom by comparing it to that of a standard atom. The result is relative mass. The **relative mass** of an atom is its mass expressed in terms of the mass of the standard atom. The isotope of the element carbon is the standard atom. It has six (6) neutrons and is called carbon-12. It is assigned a mass of 12 atomic mass units (amu). Therefore, the **atomic mass unit (amu)** is the standard unit for measuring the mass of an atom. It is equal to the mass of a carbon atom.

The **mass number** of an atom is the sum of its protons and neutrons. In any element, there is a mixture of isotopes, some having slightly more or slightly fewer protons and neutrons. The **atomic mass** of an element is an average of the mass numbers of its atoms.
The following table summarizes the terms used to describe atomic nuclei:

Term	Example	Meaning	Characteristic
Atomic Number	# protons (p)	same for all atoms of a given element	Carbon (C) atomic number = 6 (6p)
Mass number	# protons + # neutrons (p + n)	changes for different isotopes of an element	C-12 (6p + 6n) C-13 (6p + 7n)
Atomic mass	average mass of the atoms of the element	usually not a whole number	atomic mass of carbon equals 12.011

Each atom has an equal number of electrons (negative) and protons (positive). Therefore, atoms are neutral. Electrons orbiting the nucleus occupy energy levels that are arranged in order and the electrons tend to occupy the lowest energy level available. A **stable electron arrangement** is an atom that has all of its electrons in the lowest possible energy levels.

Each energy level holds a maximum number of electrons. However, an atom with more than one level does not hold more than 8 electrons in its outermost shell.

Level	Name	Max. # of Electrons
First	K shell	2
Second	L shell	8
Third	M shell	18
Fourth	N shell	32

This can help explain why chemical reactions occur. Atoms react with each other when their outer levels are unfilled. When atoms either exchange or share electrons with each other, these energy levels become filled and the atom becomes more stable.

As an electron gains energy, it moves from one energy level to a higher energy level. The electron can not leave one level until it has enough energy to reach the next level. **Excited electrons** are electrons that have absorbed energy and have moved farther from the nucleus.

Electrons can also lose energy. When they do, they fall to a lower level. However, they can only fall to the lowest level that has room for them. This explains why atoms do not collapse.

SKILL 2.8 **Identify groups of elements in the periodic table, given chemical or physical properties.**

The **periodic table of elements** is an arrangement of the elements in rows and columns so that it is easy to locate elements with similar properties. The elements of the modern periodic table are arranged in numerical order by atomic number.

The **periods** are the rows down the left side of the table. They are called first period, second period, etc. The columns of the periodic table are called **groups**, or **families.** Elements in a family have similar properties.

There are three types of elements that are grouped by color: metals, nonmetals, and metalloids.

Element Key
Atomic
Number

↓

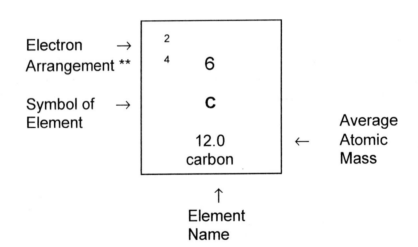

** Number of electrons on each level. Top number represents the innermost level.

SKILL 2.9   Apply knowledge of the periodic table to determine placement of elements.

The periodic table arranges metals into families with similar properties. The periodic table has its columns marked IA - VIIIA. These are the traditional group numbers. Arabic numbers 1 - 18 are also used, as suggested by the Union of Physicists and Chemists. The Arabic numerals will be used in this text.

Metals:

With the exception of hydrogen, all elements in Group 1 are **alkali metals**. These metals are shiny, softer, and less dense, and the most chemically active.

Group 2 metals are the **alkaline earth metals.** They are harder, denser, have higher melting points, and are chemically active.

The **transition elements** can be found by finding the periods (rows) from 4 to 7 under the groups (columns) 3 - 12. They are metals that do not show a range of properties as you move across the chart. They are hard and have high melting points. Compounds of these elements are colorful, such as silver, gold, and mercury.

Elements can be combined to make metallic objects. An **alloy** is a mixture of two or more elements having properties of metals. The elements do not have to be all metals. For instance, steel is made up of the metal iron and the non-metal carbon.

Nonmetals:

Nonmetals are not as easy to recognize as metals because they do not always share physical properties. However, in general the properties of nonmetals are the opposite of metals. They are not shiny, are brittle, and are not good conductors of heat and electricity.

Nonmetals are solids, gases, and one liquid (bromine).

Nonmetals have four to eight electrons in their outermost energy levels and tend to attract electrons to their outer energy levels. As a result, the outer levels usually are filled with eight electrons. This difference in the number of electrons is what caused the differences between metals and nonmetals. The outstanding chemical property of nonmetals is that react with metals.

The **halogens** can be found in Group 17. Halogens combine readily with metals to form salts. Table salt, fluoride toothpaste, and bleach all have an element from the halogen family.

The **Noble Gases** got their name from the fact that they did not react chemically with other elements, much like the nobility did not mix with the masses. These gases (found in Group 18) will only combine with other elements under very specific conditions. They are **inert** (inactive).

In recent years, scientists have found this to be only generally true, since chemists have been able to prepare compounds of krypton and xenon.

Metalloids:

Metalloids have properties in between metals and nonmetals. They can be found in Groups 13 - 16, but do not occupy the entire group. They are arranged in stair steps across the groups.

Physical Properties:
1. All are solids having the appearance of metals.
2. All are white or gray, but not shiny.
3. They will conduct electricity, but not as well as a metal.

Chemical Properties:
1. Have some characteristics of metals and nonmetals.
2. Properties do not follow patterns like metals and nonmetals. Each must be studied individually.

Boron is the first element in Group 13. It is a poor conductor of electricity at low temperatures. However, increase its temperature and it becomes a good conductor. By comparison, metals, which are good conductors, lose their ability as they are heated. It is because of this property that boron is so useful. Boron is a semiconductor. **Semiconductors** are used in electrical devices that have to function at temperatures too high for metals.

Silicon is the second element in Group 14. It is also a semiconductor and is found in great abundance in the earth's crust. Sand is made of a silicon compound, silicon dioxide. Silicon is also used in the manufacture of glass and cement.

SKILL 2.10 Compare covalent and ionic bonding

The outermost electrons in the atoms are called **valence electrons.** Because they are the ones involved in the bonding process, they determine the properties of the element.

A **chemical bond** is a force of attraction that holds atoms together. When atoms are bonded chemically, they cease to have their individual properties. For instance, hydrogen and oxygen combine into water and no longer look like hydrogen and oxygen. They look like water.

A **covalent bond** is formed when two atoms share electrons. Recall that atoms whose outer shells are not filled with electrons are unstable. When they are unstable, they readily combine with other unstable atoms. By combining and sharing electrons, they act as a single unit. Covalent bonding happens among nonmetals. Covalent bonds are always polar when between two non-identical atoms.

Covalent compounds are compounds whose atoms are joined by covalent bonds. Table sugar, methane, and ammonia are examples of covalent compounds.

An **ionic bond** is a bond formed by the transfer of electrons. It happens when metals and nonmetals bond. Before chlorine and sodium combine, the sodium has one valence electron and chlorine has seven. Neither valence shell is filled, but the chlorine's valence shell is almost full. During the reaction, the sodium gives one valence electron to the chlorine atom. Both atoms then have filled shells and are stable. Something else has happened during the bonding. Before the bonding, both atoms were neutral. When one electron was transferred, it upset the balance of protons and electrons in each atom. The chlorine atom took on one extra electron and the sodium atom released one atom. The atoms have now become ions. **Ions** are atoms with an unequal number of protons and electrons. To determine whether the ion is positive or negative, compare the number of protons (+charge) to the electrons (-charge). If there are more electrons the ion will be negative. If there are more protons, the ion will be positive.

Compounds that result from the transfer of metal atoms to nonmetal atoms are called **ionic compounds.** Sodium chloride (table salt), sodium hydroxide (drain cleaner), and potassium chloride (salt substitute) are examples of ionic compounds.

Spontaneous diffusion occurs when random motion leads particles to increase entropy by equalizing concentrations. Particles tend to move into places of lower concentration. For example, sodium will move into a cell if the concentration is greater outside than inside the cell. Spontaneous diffusion keeps cells balanced.

SKILL 2.11   Identify types of chemical reactions and their characteristics.

There are four kinds of chemical reactions:

In a **composition reaction**, two or more substances combine to form a compound.

A + B → AB
i.e. silver and sulfur yield silver dioxide

In a **decomposition reaction**, a compound breaks down into two or more simpler substances.

AB → A + B
i.e. water breaks down into hydrogen and oxygen

In a **single replacement reaction**, a free element replaces an element that is part of a compound.

A + BX → AX + B
i.e. iron plus copper sulfate yields iron sulfate plus copper

In a **double replacement reaction**, parts of two compounds replace each other. In this case, the compounds seem to switch partners.

AX + BY → AY + BX
i.e. sodium chloride plus mercury nitrate yields sodium nitrate plus mercury chloride

COMPETENCY 3.0 KNOWLEDGE OF EARTH/SPACE SCIENCE

SKILL 3.1 Explain plate tectonics theory and continental drift as each relates to geologic history or phenomena (eg., volcanism and diastrophism).

Data obtained from many sources led scientists to develop the theory of plate tectonics. This theory is the most current model that explains not only the movement of the continents, but also the changes in the earth's crust caused by internal forces.

Plates are rigid blocks of earth's crust and upper mantle. These rigid solid blocks make up the lithosphere. The earth's lithosphere is broken into nine large sections and several small ones. These moving slabs are called plates. The major plates are named after the continents they are "transporting."

The plates float on and move with a layer of hot, plastic-like rock in the upper mantle. Geologists believe that the heat currents circulating within the mantle cause this plastic zone of rock to slowly flow, carrying along the overlying crustal plates.

Movement of these crustal plates creates areas where the plates diverge as well as areas where the plates converge. In the Mid-Atlantic is a major area of divergence. Currents of hot mantle rock rise and separate at this point of divergence creating new oceanic crust at the rate of 2 to 10 centimeters per year. Convergence is when the oceanic crust collides with either another oceanic plate or a continental plate. The oceanic crust sinks forming an enormous trench and generating volcanic activity. Convergence also includes continent to continent plate collisions. When two plates slide past one another a transform fault is created.

These movements produce many major features of the earth's surface, such as mountain ranges, volcanoes, and earthquake zones. Most of these features are located at plate boundaries, where the plates interact by spreading apart, pressing together, or sliding past each other. These movements are very slow, averaging only a few centimeters a year.

Boundaries form between spreading plates where the crust is forced apart in a process called rifting. Rifting generally occurs at mid-ocean ridges. Rifting can also take place within a continent, splitting the continent into smaller, landmasses that drift away from each other, thereby forming an ocean basin (Red Sea) between them. As the seafloor spreading takes place, new material is added to the inner edges of the separating plates. In this way, the plates grow larger, and the ocean basin widens. This is the process that broke up the super continent Pangaea and created the Atlantic Ocean.

Boundaries between plates that are colliding are zones of intense crustal activity. When a plate of ocean crust collides with a plate of continental crust, the more dense oceanic plate slides under the lighter continental plate and plunges into the mantle. This process is called **subduction**, and the site where it takes place is called a subduction zone. A subduction zone is usually seen on the sea-floor as a deep depression called a trench.

The crustal movement which is characterized by plates sliding sideways past each other produces a plate boundary characterized by major faults that are capable of unleashing powerful earth-quakes. The San Andreas Fault forms such a boundary between the Pacific Plate and the North American Plate.

SKILL 3.2   Identify characteristics of geologic structures and the mechanisms by which they were formed (eg. mountains and glaciers).

Orogeny is the term given to natural mountain building.

A mountain is terrain that has been raised high above the surrounding landscape by volcanic action, or some form of tectonic plate collisions. The plate collisions could be intercontinental or ocean floor collisions with a continental crust (subduction). The physical composition of mountains would include igneous, metamorphic, or sedimentary rocks; some may have rock layers that are tilted or distorted by plate collision forces.

There are many different types of mountains. The physical attributes of a mountain range depends upon the angle at which plate movement thrust layers of rock to the surface. Many mountains (Adirondacks, Southern Rockies) were formed along high angle faults.

Folded mountains (Alps, Himalayas) are produced by the folding of rock layers during their formation. The Himalayas are the highest mountains in the world and contains Mount Everest which rises almost 9 km above sea level. The Himalayas were formed when India collided with Asia. The movement which created this collision is still in process at the rate of a few centimeters per year.

Fault-block mountains (Utah, Arizona, and New Mexico) are created when plate movement produces tension forces instead of compression forces. The area under tension produces normal faults and rock along these faults is displaced upward.

Dome mountains are formed as magma tries to push up through the crust but fails to break the surface. Dome mountains resemble a huge blister on the earth's surface.

Upwarped mountains (Black Hills of S.D.) are created in association with a broad arching of the crust. They can also be formed by rock thrust upward along high angle faults.

Volcanic mountains are built up by successive deposits of volcanic materials.

Volcanism is the term given to the movement of magma through the crust and its emergence as lava onto the earth's surface.

An active volcano is one that is presently erupting or building to an eruption. A dormant volcano is one that is between eruptions but still shows signs of internal activity that might lead to an eruption in the future. An extinct volcano is said to be no longer capable of erupting. Most of the world's active volcanoes are found along the rim of the Pacific Ocean, which is also a major earthquake zone. This curving belt of active faults and volcanoes is often called the Ring of Fire.

The world's best known volcanic mountains include: Mount Etna in Italy and Mount Kilimanjaro in Africa. The Hawaiian Islands are actually the tops of a chain of volcanic mountains that rise from the ocean floor.

There are three types of volcanic mountains: shield volcanoes, cinder cones and composite volcanoes.

Shield Volcanoes are associated with quiet eruptions. Lava emerges from the vent or opening in the crater and flows freely out over the earth's surface until it cools and hardens into a layer of igneous rock. A repeated lava flow builds this type of volcano into the largest volcanic mountain. Mauna Loa found in Hawaii, is the largest volcano on earth.

Cinder Cone Volcanoes associated with explosive eruptions as lava is hurled high into the air in a spray of droplets of various sizes. These droplets cool and harden into cinders and particles of ash before falling to the ground. The ash and cinder pile up around the vent to form a steep, cone-shaped hill called the cinder cone. Cinder cone volcanoes are relatively small but may form quite rapidly.

Composite Volcanoes are described as being built by both lava flows and layers of ash and cinders. Mount Fuji in Japan, Mount St. Helens in Washington, USA and Mount Vesuvius in Italy are all famous Composite Volcanoes.

Mechanisms of producing mountains

Mountains are produced by different types of mountain-building processes. Most major mountain ranges are formed by the processes of folding and faulting.

Folded Mountains are produced by folding of rock layers. Crustal movements may press horizontal layers of sedimentary rock together from the sides, squeezing them into wavelike folds. Up-folded sections of rock are called anticlines; down-folded sections of rock are called synclines. The Appalachian Mountains are an example of folded mountains with long ridges and valleys in a series of anticlines and synclines formed by folded rock layers.

Faults are fractures in the earth's crust which have been created by either tension or compression forces transmitted through the crust. These forces are produced by the movement of separate blocks of crust.

Faultings are categorized on the basis of the relative movement between the blocks on both sides of the fault plane. The movement can be horizontal, vertical or oblique.

A dip-slip fault occurs when the movement of the plates is vertical and opposite. The displacement is in the direction of the inclination, or dip, of the fault. Dip-slip faults are classified as normal faults when the rock above the fault plane moves down relative to the rock below.

Reverse faults are created when the rock above the fault plane moves up relative to the rock below. Reverse faults having a very low angle to the horizontal are also referred to as thrust faults.

Faults in which the dominant displacement horizontal movement along the trend or strike (length) of the fault, are called strike-slip faults. When a large strike-slip fault is associated with plate boundaries it is called a transform fault. The San Andreas Fault in California is a well-known transform fault.

Faults that have both vertical and horizontal movement are called oblique-slip faults.

When lava cools, igneous rock is formed. This formation can occur either above ground or below ground.

Intrusive rock includes any igneous rock that was formed below the earth's surface. Batholiths are the largest structures of intrusive type rock and are composed of near granite materials; they are the core of the Sierra Nevada Mountains.

Extrusive rock includes any igneous rock that was formed at the earth's surface

Dikes are old lava tubes formed when magma entered a vertical fracture and hardened. Sometimes magma squeezes between two rock layers and hardens into a thin horizontal sheet called a sill. A **laccolith** is formed in much the same way as a sill, but the magma that creates a **laccolith** is very thick and does not flow easily. It pools and forces the overlying strat creating an obvious surface dome.

A **caldera** is normally formed by the collapse of the top of a volcano. This collapse can be caused by a massive explosion that destroys the cone and empties most if not all of the magma chamber below the volcano. The cone collapses into the empty magma chamber forming a caldera.

An inactive volcano may have magma solidified in its pipe. This structure, called a volcanic neck, is resistant to erosion and today may be the only visible evidence of the past presence of an active volcano.

When lava cools, igneous rock is formed. This formation can occur either above ground or below ground.

Glaciation

A continental glacier covered a large part of North America during the most recent ice age. Evidence of this glacial coverage remains as abrasive grooves, large boulders from northern environments dropped in southerly locations, glacial troughs created by the rounding out of steep valleys by glacial scouring, and the remains of glacial sources called **cirques** that were created by frost wedging the rock at the bottom of the glacier. Remains of plants and animals found in warm climate have been discovered in the moraines and out wash plains help to support the theory of periods of warmth during the past ice ages.

The Ice Age began about 2 -3 million years ago. This age saw the advancement and retreat of glacial ice over millions of years. Theories relating to the origin of glacial activity include Plate Tectonics where it can be demonstrated that some continental masses, now in temperate climates, were at one time blanketed by ice and snow. Another theory involves changes in the earth's orbit around the sun, changes in the angle of the earth's axis, and the wobbling of the earth's axis. Support for the validity of this theory has come from deep ocean research that indicates a correlation between climatic sensitive micro-organisms and the changes in the earth's orbital status.

About 12,000 years ago, a vast sheet of ice covered a large part of the northern United States. This huge, frozen mass had moved southward from the northern regions of Canada as several large bodies of slow-moving ice, or glaciers. A time period in which glaciers advance over a large portion of a continent is called an ice age. A glacier is a large mass of ice that moves or flows over the land in response to gravity. Glaciers form among high mountains and in other cold regions.

There are two main types of glaciers: valley glaciers and continental glaciers. Erosion by valley glaciers is characteristic of U-shaped erosion. They produce sharp peaked mountains such as the Matterhorn in Switzerland. Erosion by continental glaciers often rides over mountains in their paths leaving smoothed, rounded mountains and ridges.

SKILL 3.3   Explain the formation of fossils and how they are used to interpret the past.

The fossil is the remains or trace of an ancient organism that has been preserved naturally in the Earth's crust. Sedimentary rocks usually are rich sources of fossil remains. Those fossils found in layers of sediment were embedded in the slowly forming sedimentary rock strata. The oldest fossils known are the traces of 3.5 billion year old bacteria found in sedimentary rocks. Few fossils are found in metamorphic rock and virtually none found in igneous rocks. The magma is so hot that any organism trapped in the magma is destroyed.

The fossil remains of a woolly mammoth embedded in ice were found by a group of Russian explorers. However, the best-preserved animal remains have been discovered in natural tar pits. When an animal accidentally fell into the tar, it became trapped sinking to the bottom. Preserved bones of the saber-toothed cat have been found in tar pits.

Prehistoric insects have been found trapped in ancient amber or fossil resin that was excreted by some extinct species of pine trees.

Fossil molds are the hollow spaces in a rock previously occupied by bones or shells. A fossil cast is a fossil mold that fills with sediments or minerals that later hardens forming a cast.

Fossil tracks are the imprints in harden mud left behind by the birds or animals.

SKILL 3.4   Identify the order of geologic time periods, life forms present in each period and methods for determining geologic age.

The biological history of the earth is partitioned into four major Eras which are further divided into major periods. The latter periods are refined into groupings called Epochs.

Earth's history extends over more than four billion years and is reckoned in terms of a scale. Paleontologists who study the history of the Earth have divided this huge period of time into four large time units called eons. Eons are divided into smaller units of time called eras. An era refers to a time interval in which particular plants and animals were dominant, or present in great abundance. The end of an era is most often characterized by (1) a general uplifting of the crust, (2) the extinction of the dominant plants or animals, and (3) the appearance of new life-forms.

Each era is divided into several smaller divisions of time called periods. Some periods are divided into smaller time units called epochs.

Methods of geologic dating

Estimates of the Earth's age have been made possible with the discovery of **radioactivity** and the invention of instruments that can measure the amount of radioactivity in rocks. The use of radioactivity to make accurate determinations of Earth's age is called Absolute Dating. This process depends upon comparing the amount of radioactive material in a rock with the amount that has decayed into another element. Studying the radiation given off by atoms of radioactive elements is the most accurate method of measuring the Earth's age. These atoms are unstable and are continuously breaking down or undergoing decay. The radioactive element that decays is called the parent element. The new element that results from the radioactive decay of the parent element is called the daughter element.

The time required for one half of a given amount of a radioactive element to decay is called the half-life of that element or compound.

Geologists commonly use Carbon Dating to calculate the age of a fossil substance.

Infer the history of an area using geologic evidence

The determination of the age of rocks by cataloging their composition has been outmoded since the middle 1800s. Today a sequential history can be determined by the fossil content (principle of fossil succession) of a rock system as well as its superposition within a range of systems. This classification process was termed stratigraphy and permitted the construction of a Geologic Column in which rock systems are arranged in their correct chronological order.

Principles of catastrophism and uniformitarianism

Uniformitarianism - is a fundamental concept in modern geology. It simply states that the physical, chemical, and biological laws that operated in the geologic past operate in the same way today. The forces and processes that we observe presently shaping our planet have been at work for a very long time. This idea is commonly stated as "the present is the key to the past."

Catastrophism - the concept that the earth was shaped by catastrophic events of a short term nature.

> **SKILL 3.5**   **Interpret various geologic maps, including topographic and weather maps that contain symbols, scales, legends, directions, time zones, latitudes, and longitudes.**

Decode map symbols

Hachures are depressions or tiny comb-like markings that point inward from the contour line toward the bottom of the depression. A contour line that has hachures is called a depression contour.

A system of imaginary lines has been developed that helps people describe exact locations on Earth. Looking at a globe of Earth, you will see lines drawn on it. The equator is drawn around Earth halfway between the North and South Poles. Latitude is a term used to describe distance in degrees north or south of the equator. Lines of latitude are drawn east and west parallel to the equator. Degrees of latitude range from 0 at the equator to 90 at either the North Pole or South Pole. Lines of latitude are also called parallels.

Lines drawn north and south at right angles to the equator and from pole to pole are called meridians. Longitude is a term used to describe distances in degrees east or west of a 0° meridian. The prime meridian is the 0° meridian and it passes through Greenwich, England.

Time zones are determined by longitudinal lines. Each time zone represents one hour. Since there are 24 hours in one complete rotation of the Earth, there are 24 international time zones. Each time zone is roughly 15° wide. While time zones are based on meridians, they do not strictly follow lines of longitude. Time zone boundaries are subject to political decisions and have been moved around cities and other areas at the whim of the electorate.

The International Date Line is the 180° meridian and it is on the opposite side of the world from the prime meridian. The International Date Line is one-half of one day or 12 time zones from the prime meridian. If you were traveling west across the International Date Line, you would lose one day. If you were traveling east across the International Date Line, you would gain one day.

Principles of contouring

A contour line is a line on a map representing an imaginary line on the ground that has the same elevation above sea level along its entire length. Contour intervals usually are given in even numbers or as a multiple of five. In mapping mountains, a large contour interval is used. Small contour intervals may be used where there are small differences in elevation.

Relief describes how much variation in elevation an area has. Rugged or high relief, describes an area of many hills and valleys. Gentle or low relief describes a plain area or a coastal region. Five general rules should be remembered in studying contour lines on a map.

1. Contour lines close around hills and basins or depressions. Hachure lines are used to show depressions. Hachures are short lines placed at right angles to the contour line and they always point toward the lower elevation.

2. Contours lines never cross. Contour lines are sometimes very close together. Each contour line represents a certain height above sea level.

3. Contour lines appear on both sides of an area where the slope reverses direction. Contour lines show where an imaginary horizontal plane would slice through a hillside or cut both sides of a valley.

4. Contours lines form V's that point upstream when they cross streams. Streams cut beneath the general elevation of the land surface, and contour lines follow a valley.

5. All contours lines either close (connect) or extend to the edge of the map. No map is large enough to have all its contour lines close.

Interpret maps and imagery

Like photographs, maps readily display information that would be impractical to express in words. Maps that show the shape of the land are called topographic maps. Topographic maps, which are also referred to as quadrangles, are generally classified according to publication scale. Relief refers to the difference in elevation between any two points. Maximum relief refers to the difference in elevation between the high test and lowest points in the area being considered. Relief determines the contour interval, which is the difference in elevation between succeeding contour lines that are used on topographic maps.

Map scales express the relationship between distance or area on the map to the true distance or area on the earth's surface. It is expressed as so many feet, (miles, meters, km, or degrees) per inch (cm), of map.

SKILL 3.6 Identify types of currents and tides and how each is produced.

World weather patterns are greatly influenced by ocean surface currents in the upper layer of the ocean. These current continuously move along the ocean surface in specific directions. Ocean currents that flow deep below the surface are called sub-surface currents. These currents are influenced by such factors as the location of landmasses in the current's path and the earth's rotation.

Surface currents are caused by winds and classified by temperature. Cold currents originate in the Polar regions and flow through surrounding water that is measurably warmer. Those currents with a higher temperature than the surrounding water are called warm currents and can be found near the equator. These currents follow swirling routes around the ocean basins and the equator. The Gulf Stream and the California Current are the two main surface currents that flow along the coastlines of the United States. The Gulf Stream is a warm current in the Atlantic Ocean that carries warm water from the equator to the northern parts of the Atlantic Ocean. Benjamin Franklin studied and named the Gulf Stream. The California Current is a cold currant that originates in the Arctic regions and flows southward along the west coast of the United States.

Differences in water density also create ocean currents. Water found near the bottom of oceans is the coldest and the densest. Water tends to flow from a denser area to a less dense area. These currents that flow because of a difference in the density of the ocean water are called density currents. Water with a higher salinity is denser than water with a lower salinity. Water that has salinity different from the surrounding water may form a density current.

Knowledge of the causes and effects of waves

The movement of ocean water is caused by the wind, the sun's heat energy, the earth's rotation, the moon's gravitational pull on earth and by underwater earthquakes. Most ocean waves are caused by the impact of winds. Wind blowing over the surface of the ocean transfers energy (friction) to the water and causes waves to form. Waves are also formed by a seismic activity on the ocean floor. A wave formed by an earthquake is called a seismic sea wave. These powerful waves can be very destructive, with wave heights increasing to 30 m or more near the shore. The crest of a wave is its highest point. The trough of a wave is its lowest point. The distance from wave top to wave top is the wavelength. The wave period is the time between the passings of two successive waves.

GENERAL SCIENCE

SKILL 3.7   Identify characteristics of the seafloor, shorelines, estuaries, and sea zones.

Seafloor

The ocean floor has many of the same features that are found on land. The ocean floor has higher mountains than present on land, extensive plains and deeper canyons than present on land. Oceanographers have named different parts of the ocean floor according to their structure.
The major parts of the ocean floor are:

The **continental shelf** is the sloping part of the continent that is covered with water extending from the shoreline to the continental slope.

The **continental slope** is the steeply sloping area that connects the continental shelf and the deep-ocean floor.

The **continental rise** is the gently sloping surface at the base of the continental slope.

The **abyssal plains** are the flat, level parts of the ocean floor.

A **seamount** is an undersea volcano peak that is at least 1000 m above the ocean floor.

Guyot - A submerged flat-topped seamount

Mid ocean-ridges are continuous undersea mountain chains that are found mostly in the middle portions of the oceans.

Ocean trenches are long, elongated narrow troughs or depressions formed where ocean floors collide with another section of ocean floor or continent. The deepest trench in the Pacific Ocean is the Marianas Trench which is about 11 km deep.

Shorelines

The shoreline is the boundary where land and sea meet. Shorelines mark the average position of sea level, which is the average height of the sea without consideration of tides and waves. Shorelines are classified according to the way they were formed. The three types of shorelines are: submerged, emergent, and neutral. When the sea has risen, or the land has sunk, a **submerged shoreline** is created. An **emergent shoreline** occurs when sea falls or the land rises. A **neutral shoreline** does not show the features of a submerged or an emergent shoreline. A neutral shoreline is usually observed as a flat and broad beach.

A **stack** is an island of resistant rock left after weaker rock is worn away by waves and currents. Waves approaching the beach at a slight angle create a current of water that flows parallel to the shore. This longshore current carries loose sediment almost like a river of sand. A spit is formed when a weak longshore current drops its load of sand as it turns into a bay.

Rip currents are narrow currents that flow seaward at a right angle to the shoreline. These currents are very dangerous to swimmers. Most of the beach sands are composed of grains of resistant material like quartz and orthoclase but coral or basalt are found in some locations. Many beaches have rock fragments that are too large to be classified as sand.

SKILL 3.8   Identify the chemical and physical properties of ocean water.

Seventy percent of the earth's surface is covered with saltwater which is termed the hydrosphere. The mass of this saltwater is about 1.4×10^{24} grams. The ocean waters continuously circulate among different parts of the hydrosphere. There are seven major oceans: the North Atlantic Ocean, South Atlantic Ocean, North Pacific Ocean, South Pacific Ocean, Indian Ocean, Arctic Ocean, and the Antarctic Ocean.

Pure water is a combination of the elements hydrogen and oxygen. These two elements make up about 96.5% of the ocean water. The remaining portion is made up of dissolved solids. The concentration of these dissolved solids determines the water's salinity.

Salinity is the number of grams of these dissolved salts in 1,000 grams of sea water. The average salinity of ocean water is about 3.5%. In other words, one kilogram of sea water contains about 35 grams of salt. Sodium Chloride or salt (NaCl) is the most abundant of the dissolved salts. The dissolved salts also include smaller quantities of magnesium chloride, magnesium and calcium sulfates, and traces of several other salt elements. Salinity varies throughout the world oceans; the total salinity of the oceans varies from place to place and also varies with depth. Salinity is low near river mouths where the ocean mixes with fresh water, and salinity is high in areas of high evaporation rates.

The temperature of the ocean water varies with different latitudes and with ocean depths. Ocean water temperature is about constant to depths of 90 meters (m). The temperature of surface water will drop rapidly from 28° C at the equator to -2° C at the Poles. The freezing point of sea water is lower than the freezing point of pure water. Pure water freezes at 0° C. The dissolved salts in the sea water keep sea water at a freezing point of -2° C. The freezing point of sea water may vary depending on its salinity in a particular location.

The ocean can be divided into three temperature zones. The surface layer consists of relatively warm water and exhibits most of the wave action present. The area where the wind and waves churn and mix the water is called the mixed layer. This is the layer where most living creatures are found due to abundant sunlight and warmth. The second layer is called the thermocline and it becomes increasingly cold as its depth increases. This change is due to the lack of energy from sunlight. The layer below the thermocline continues to the deep dark, very cold, and semi-barren ocean floor.

Oozes - the name given to the sediment that contains at least 30% plant or animal shell fragments. Ooze contains calcium carbonate. Deposits that form directly from sea water in the place where they are found are called:

Authigenic deposits- maganese nodules are authigenic deposits found over large areas of the ocean floor.

Causes for the formation of ocean floor features.

The surface of the earth is in constant motion. This motion is the subject of Plate Tectonics studies. Major plate separation lines lie along the ocean floors. As these plates separate, molten rock rises, continuously forming new ocean crust and creating new and taller mountain ridges under the ocean. The Mid-Atlantic Range, which divides the Atlantic Ocean basin into two nearly equal parts, shows evidence from mapping of these deep-ocean floor changes.

Seamounts are formed by underwater volcanoes. Seamounts and volcanic islands are found in long chains on the ocean floor. They are formed when the movement of an oceanic plate positions a plate section over a stationary hot spot located deep in the mantle. Magma rising from the hot spot punches through the plate and forms a volcano. The Hawaiian Islands are examples of volcanic island chains.

Magma that rises to produce a curving chain of volcanic islands is called an island arc. An example of an island arc is the Lesser Antilles chain in the Caribbean Sea.

SKILL 3.9 Identify the major groups of rocks and processes by which each is formed.

Three major subdivisions of rocks are sedimentary, metamorphic and igneous.

Lithification of sedimentary rocks

When fluid sediments are transformed into solid sedimentary rocks, the process is known as lithification. One very common process affecting sediments is compaction where the weights of overlying materials compress and compact the deeper sediments. The compaction process leads to cementation. **Cementation** is when sediments are converted to sedimentary rock.

Factors in crystallization of igneous rocks

Igneous rocks can be classified: according to their texture, their composition, and the way they formed.

Molten rock is called magma. When molten rock pours out onto the surface of Earth, it is called lava.

As magma cools, the elements and compounds begin to form crystals. The slower the magma cools, the larger the crystals grow. Rocks with large crystals are said to have a coarse-grained texture. Granite is an example of a coarse grained rock. Rocks that cool rapidly before any crystals can form have a glassy texture such as obsidian, also commonly known as volcanic glass.

Metamorphic rocks are formed by high temperatures and great pressures. The process by which the rocks undergo these changes is called metamorphism. The outcome of metamorphic changes include deformation by extreme heat and pressure, compaction, destruction of the original characteristics of the parent rock, bending and folding while in a plastic stage, and the emergence of completely new and different minerals due to chemical reactions with heated water and dissolved minerals.

Metamorphic rocks are classified into two groups, foliated (leaflike) rocks and unfoliated rocks. Foliated rocks consist of compressed, parallel bands of minerals, which give the rocks a striped appearance. Examples of such rocks include; slate, schist, and gneiss. Unfoliated rocks are not banded and examples of such include; quartzite, marble, and anthracite rocks.

Minerals are natural, non-living solids with a definite chemical composition and a crystalline structure. **Ores** are minerals or rock deposits that can be mined for a profit. **Rocks** are Earth materials made of one or more minerals. **Rock Facies** is a rock group that differs from comparable rocks (as in composition, age or fossil content).

GENERAL SCIENCE

Characteristics by which minerals are classified.

Minerals must adhere to five criteria. They must be   (1) non-living, (2) formed in nature, (3) solid in form, (4) their atoms form a crystalline pattern,   (5) Its chemical composition is fixed within narrow limits.

There are over 3000 minerals in earth's crust. Minerals are classified by composition. The major groups of minerals are silicates, carbonates, oxides, sulfides, sulfates, and halides. The largest group of minerals is the silicates. Silicates are made of silicon, oxygen, and one or more other elements.

SKILL 3.10   Knowledge of soil types and properties.

Soils are composed of particles of sand, clay, various minerals, tiny living organisms, and humus, plus the decayed remains of plants and animals. Soils are divided into three classes according to their texture. These classes are sandy soils, clay soils, and loamy soils.

Sandy soils are gritty, and their particles do not bind together firmly. Sandy soils are porous - water passes through them rapidly. Sandy soils do not hold much water.

Clay soils are smooth and greasy, their particles bind together firmly. Clay soils are moist and usually do not allow water to pass through easily.

Loamy soils feel somewhat like velvet and their particles clump together. Loamy soils are made up of sand, clay, and silt. Loamy soils holds water but some water can pass through.

Soils are grouped into three major types based upon their composition, pedalfers, pedocals and laterites.

Pedalfers form in the humid, temperate climate of the eastern United States. Pedalfer soils contain large amounts of iron oxide and aluminum-rich clays, making the soil a brown to reddish brown color. This soil supports forest type vegetation.

Pedocals are found in the western United States where the climate is dry and temperate. These soils are rich in calcium carbonate. This type of soil supports grasslands and brush vegetation.
Laterites are found where the climate is wet and tropical. Large amounts of water flows through this soil. Laterites are red-orange soils rich in iron and aluminum oxides. There is little humus and this soil is not very fertile.

SKILL 3.11 Identify renewable and nonrenewable natural resources.

A **renewable resource** is one that is replaced naturally. Living renewable resources would be plants and animals. Plants are renewable because they grow and reproduce. Sometimes renewal of the resource doesn't keep up with the demand. Such is the case with trees. Since the housing industry uses lumber for frames and homebuilding they are often cut down faster than new trees can grow. Now there are specific tree farms. Special methods allow trees to grow faster.

A second renewable resource is animals. They renew by the process of reproduction. Some wild animals need protection on refuges. As the population of humans increases resources are used faster. Cattle are used for their hides and for food. Some animals like deer are killed for sport. Each state has an environmental protection agency with divisions of forest management and wildlife management.

Non-living renewable resources would be water, air, and soil. Water is renewed in a natural cycle called the water cycle. Air is a mixture of gases. Oxygen is given off by plants and taken in by animals that in turn expel the carbon dioxide that the plants need. Soil is another renewable resource. Fertile soil is rich in minerals. When plants grow they remove the minerals and make the soil less fertile. Chemical treatments are one way or renewing the composition. It is also accomplished naturally when the plants decay back into the soil. The plant material is used to make compost to mix with the soil.

Nonrenewable resources are not easily replaced in a timely fashion. Minerals are nonrenewable resources. Quartz, mica, salt and sulfur are some examples. Mining depletes these resources so society may benefit by glass from quartz, electronic equipment from mica, and salt has many uses. Sulfur is used in medicine, fertilizers, paper, and matches.

Metals are among the most widely used nonrenewable resource. Metals must be separated from the ore. Iron is our most important ore. Gold, silver and copper are often found in a more pure form called native metals.

GENERAL SCIENCE

SKILL 3.12 Apply knowledge of the processes of erosion, weathering, transportation and deposition.

Erosion is the inclusion and transportation of surface materials by another moveable material, usually water, wind, or ice. The most important cause of erosion is running water. Streams, rivers, tides and such are constantly at work removing weathered fragments of bedrock and carrying them away from their original location.

A stream erodes bedrock by the grinding action of the sand, pebbles and other rock fragments. This grinding against each other is called abrasion.

Streams also erode rocks by the dissolving or absorbing their minerals. Limestone and marble are readily dissolved by streams.

The breaking down of rocks at or near to the earth's surface is known as **weathering**. Weathering breaks down these rocks into smaller and smaller pieces. There are two types of weathering, physical weathering and chemical weathering.

Physical weathering is the process by which rocks are broken down into smaller fragments without undergoing any change in chemical composition. Physical weathering is mainly caused by the freezing of water, the expansion of rock, and the activities of plants and animals.

Frost wedging is the cycle of daytime thawing and refreezing at night. This cycle causes large rock masses, especially the rocks exposed on mountain tops, to be broken into smaller pieces.

The peeling away of the outer layers from a rock is called exfoliation. Rounded mountain tops are called exfoliation domes and have been formed in this way.

Chemical weathering is the breaking down of rocks through changes in their chemical composition. An example would be the change of feldspar in granite to clay. Water, oxygen, and carbon dioxide are the main agents of chemical weathering. When water and carbon dioxide combine chemically, they produce a weak acid that breaks down rocks.

SKILL 3.13   Identify characteristics of the sun and other stars and devices and techniques for collecting data about stars.

The **sun** is considered the nearest star to earth that produces solar energy by the process of nuclear fusion, hydrogen gas is converted to helium gas. Energy flows out of the core to the surface, radiation then escapes into space.

Parts of the sun include: (1) **core**, the inner portion of the sun where fusion takes place, (2) **photosphere**, considered the surface of the sun which produces **sunspots** (cool, dark areas that can be seen on its surface), (3) **chromosphere**, hydrogen gas causes this portion to be red in color, **solar flares** (sudden brightness of the chromosphere) and **solar prominences** (gases that shoot outward from the chromosphere) is found in the chromosphere, and (4) **corona**, the transparent area of sun visible only during a total eclipse.

Solar radiation is energy traveling from the sun that radiates into space. **Solar flares** produce excited protons and electrons that shoot outward from the chromosphere at great speeds reaching earth. These particles disturb radio reception and also affect the magnetic field on earth.

Knowledge of telescope types

Galilee was the first person to use telescopes to observer the solar system. He invented the first refracting telescope. A **refracting telescope** uses lenses to bend light rays in focusing the image.

Sir Isaac Newton invented the **reflecting telescope** using mirrors to gather light rays on a curved mirror which produces a small focused image.

The world's largest telescope is located in Mauna Kea, Hawaii. It uses multiple-mirrors to gather light rays.

The **Hubble Space telescope** uses a **single-reflector mirror**. It provides an opportunity for astronomers to observe objects seven times farther away even those objects that are 50 times fainter better than any other telescope on earth. There are future plans to make repairs and install new mirrors and other equipment on the Hubble Space telescope.

Refracting and reflecting telescopes are considered **optical telescopes** since they gather visible light and focus it to produce images. A different type of telescope that collects invisible radio waves created by the sun and stars is called a **radio telescope.**

GENERAL SCIENCE

Radio telescopes consists of a reflector or dish with special receivers. The reflector collects radio waves that are created by the sun and stars. There are many advantages using a radio telescope; they can receive signals 24 hours a day, can operate in any kind of weather, dust particles or clouds does not interfere with its performance. The most impressive aspect of the radio telescope is its ability to detect objects from such great distances in space.

The world's largest radio telescope is located in Arecibo, Puerto Rico. It has a collecting dish antenna of more than 300 meters in diameter.

Use spectral analysis to identify or infer features of stars or star systems.

The **spectroscope** is a device or an attachment for telescopes that is used to separate white light into a series different color by wave lengths. This series of colors of light is called a **spectrum**. A **spectrograph** can photograph a spectrum. Wavelengths of light have distinctive colors. The color red has the longest wavelength and violet has the shortest wavelength. Wavelengths are arranged to form an **electromagnetic spectrum**, (see figure 3.18a) they range from very long radio waves to very short gamma rays. Visible light covers a small portion of the electromagnetic spectrum. Spectroscopes observe the spectra, temperatures, pressures, and also the movement of stars. The movements of stars indicate if they are moving toward or away from earth.

If a star is moving towards earth, light waves compress and the wavelengths of light seem shorter. This will cause the entire spectrum to move towards the blue or violet end of the spectrum. This spectral shift to the blue or violet spectrum observed on the electromagnetic spectrum.

If a star is moving away from earth, light waves expand and the wavelengths of light seem longer. This will cause the entire spectrum to move towards the red end of the spectrum. This spectral shift to the red spectrum is observed on the electromagnetic spectrum.

Knowledge of astronomical measurement.

The three formulas astronomers use for calculating distances in space are: (1) the **AU or astronomical unit**, (2) **the LY or Light year,** and (3) **the parsec**. It is important to remember that these formulas are measured in distances not measured for time.

The distance between the earth and the sun is about 150×10^6 km. This distance is known as an astronomical unit or AU. This formula is used to measure distances within the solar system, it is not used to measure time.

The distance light travels in one year, a light year or 9.5×10^{12} km. This formula is used to measure distances in space, it does not measure time.

Large distances are measured in parsecs. One parsec equals 3.26 light-years, not time.

There are approximately 63,000 AU's in one light year or,

9.5×10^{12} km$/ 150 \times 10^{6}$ km $= 6.3 \times 10^{4}$ AU

SKILL 3.14 Identify the components of the solar system and their characteristics and relationships to each other.

There are nine planets in our solar system; Mercury, Venus, Earth, Mars, Jupiter, Saturn, Uranus, Neptune, and Pluto. These nine planets are divided into two groups based on distance from the sun. The inner planets include: Mercury, Venus, Earth, and Mars. The outer planets include: Jupiter, Saturn, Uranus, Neptune and Pluto.

Planets

Mercury -- the closest planet to the sun. Its surface has craters and rocks. The atmosphere is composed of hydrogen, helium and sodium. Mercury was named after the Roman messenger god.

Venus -- has a slow rotation when compared to Earth. Venus and Uranus rotate in opposite directions from the other planets. This opposite rotation is called retrograde rotation. The surface of Venus is not visible due to the extensive cloud cover. The atmosphere is composed mostly of carbon dioxide. Sulfuric acid droplet in the dense cloud cover gives Venus a yellow appearance. Venus has a greater greenhouse effect than observed on Earth. The dense clouds Combined with carbon dioxide traps heat. Venus was named after the Roman goddess of love.

Earth -- considered a water planet with 70% of its surface covered with water. Gravity holds the masses of water in place. The different temperatures observed on earth allows for the different states of water to exist; solid, liquid or gas. The atmosphere is composed mainly of oxygen and nitrogen. Earth is the only planet that is known to support life.

Mars -- the surface of Mars contains numerous craters, active and extinct volcanoes, ridges and valleys with extremely deep fractures. Iron oxide found in the dusty soil makes the surface seem rust colored and the skies seem pink in color. The atmosphere is composed of carbon dioxide, nitrogen, argon, oxygen and water vapor. Mars has polar regions with ice caps composed of water. Mars has two satellites. Mars was named after the Roman war god.

Jupiter -- largest planet in the solar system. Jupiter has 16 moons. The atmosphere is composed of hydrogen, helium, methane and ammonia. There are white colored bands of clouds indicating rising gas and dark colored bands of clouds indicating descending gases, caused by heat resulting from the energy of Jupiter's core. Jupiter has a Great Red Spot that is thought to be a hurricane type cloud. Jupiter has a strong magnetic field.

Saturn -- the second largest planet in the solar system. Saturn has beautiful rings of ice and rock and dust particles circling it. Saturn's atmosphere is composed of hydrogen, helium, methane, and ammonia. Saturn has 20 plus satellites. Saturn was named after the Roman god of agriculture.

Uranus -- the second largest planet in the solar system with retrograde revolution. Uranus a gaseous planet and it has 10 dark rings and 15 satellites. Its atmosphere is composed of hydrogen, helium, and methane. Uranus was named after the Greek god of the heavens.

Neptune -- another gaseous planet with an atmosphere consisting of hydrogen, helium, and methane. Neptune has 3 rings and 2 satellites. Neptune was named after the Roman sea god that its atmosphere has the same color of the seas.

Pluto -- considered the smallest planet in the solar system. Pluto's atmosphere probably contains methane, ammonia, and frozen water. Pluto has 1 satellite. Pluto revolves around the sun every 250 years. Pluto was named after the Roman god of the underworld.

Comets, asteroids, and meteors.
Astronomers believe that the rocky fragments that may have been the remains of the birth of the solar system that never formed into a planet. **Asteroids** are found in the region between Mars and Jupiter.

Comets are masses of frozen gases, cosmic dust, and small rocky particles. Astronomers think that most comets originate in a dense comet cloud beyond Pluto. Comet consists of a nucleus, a coma, and a tail. A comet's tail always points away from the sun. The most famous comet, **Halley's Comet,** is named after the person whom first discovered it in 240 B.C. It returns to the skies near earth every 75 to 76 years.

Meteoroids are composed of particles of rock and metal of various sizes. When a meteoroid travels through the earth's atmosphere, friction causes its surface to heat up and it begins to burn. The burning meteoroid falling through the earth's atmosphere is now called a **meteor** or also known as a "shooting star."
Meteorites are meteors that strike the earth's surface. A physical example of the impact of the meteorite on the earth's surface can be seen in Arizona, The Barringer Crater is a huge Meteor Crater. There many other such meteor craters found throughout the world.

SKILL 3.15 Identify structures in the universe (stars, galaxies, quasars) their characteristics and their formation.

Astronomers use groups or patterns of stars called **constellations** as reference points to locate other stars in the sky. Familiar constellations include: Ursa Major (also known as the big bear) and Ursa Minor (known as the little bear). Within the Ursa Major, the smaller constellation, The Big Dipper is found. Within the Ursa Minor, the smaller constellation, The Little Dipper is found.

Different constellations appear as the earth continues its revolution around the sun with the seasonable changes.

Magnitude stars are 21 of the brightest stars that can be seen from earth, these are the first stars noticed at night. In the Northern Hemisphere there are 15 commonly observed first magnitude stars.

A vast collection of stars is defined as **galaxies**. Galaxies are classified as irregular, elliptical, and spiral. An irregular galaxy has no real structured appearance; most are in their early stages of life. An elliptical galaxy is smooth ellipses, containing little dust and gas, but composed of millions or trillion stars. Spiral galaxies are disk-shaped and have extending arms that rotate around its dense center. Earth's galaxy is found in the Milky Way and it is a spiral galaxy.

Terms related to deep space

A **pulsar** is defined as a variable radio source that emits signals in very short, regular bursts; believed to be a rotating neutron star.

A **quasar** is defined as an object that photographs like a star but has an extremely large redshift and a variable energy output; believed to be the active core of a very distant galaxy.

Black holes are defined as an object that has collapsed to such a degree that light can not escape from its surface; light is trapped by the intense gravitational field.

SKILL 3.16 Knowledge of hypotheses related to the origin of the solar system.

Two main hypotheses of the origin of the solar system are: (1) **the tidal hypothesis** and (2) **the condensation hypothesis**.

The tidal hypothesis proposes that the solar system began with a near collision of the sun and a large star. Some astronomers believe that as these two stars passed each other, the great gravitational pull of the large star extracted hot gases out of the sun. The mass from the hot gases started to orbit the sun, which began to cool then condensing into the nine planets. (Few astronomers support this example).

The condensation hypothesis proposes that the solar system began with rotating clouds of dust and gas. Condensation occurred in the center forming the sun and the smaller parts of the cloud formed the nine planets. (This example is widely accepted by many astronomers).

Two main theories to explain the origins of the universe include: (1) **The Big Bang Theory and** (2) **The Steady-State Theory.**

The Big Bang Theory has been widely accepted by many astronomers. It states that the universe originated from a magnificent explosion spreading mass, matter and energy into space.   The galaxies formed from this material as it cooled during the next half-billion years.

The Steady-State Theory is the least accepted theory. It states that the universe is a continuously being renewed. Galaxies move outward and new galaxies replace the older galaxies. Astronomers have not found any evidence to prove this theory.

The future of the universe is hypothesized with the Oscillating Universe Hypothesis. It states that the universe will oscillate or expand and contract. Galaxies will move away from one another and will in time slow down and stop. Then a gradual moving toward each other will again activate the explosion or The Big Bang theory.

SKILL 3.17   Identify components of biogeochemical cycles (eg. carbon, oxygen, hydrogen, and nitrogen) and the order in which they occur.

See section 4.21

SKILL 3.18   Identify characteristics and composition of air and atmospheric conditions (eg. air masses, wind patterns, cloud types, and storms).

El Niño refers to a sequence of changes in the ocean and atmospheric circulation across the Pacific Ocean. The water around the equator is unusually hot every two to seven years. Trade winds normally blowing east to west across the equatorial latitudes, piling warm water into the western Pacific. A huge mass of heavy thunderstorms usually forms in the area and produce vast currents of rising air that displace heat poleward. This helps create the strong mid-latitude jet streams. The world's climate patterns are disrupted by this change in location of the massive cluster of thunderstorms. The West coast of America experienced a wet winter. Sacramento, California recorded 103 days of rain.

Air masses moving toward or away from the Earth's surface are called air currents. Air moving parallel to Earth's surface is called **wind**. Weather conditions are generated by winds and air currents carrying large amounts of heat and moisture from one part of the atmosphere to another. Wind speeds are measured by instruments called anemometers.

The wind belts in each hemisphere consist of convection cells that encircle Earth like belts. There are three major wind belts on Earth (1) trade winds (2) prevailing westerlies, and (3) polar easterlies. Wind belt formation depends on the differences in air pressures that develop in the doldrums, the horse latitudes, and the polar regions. The Doldrums surround the equator. Within this belt heated air usually rises straight up into Earth's atmosphere. The Horse latitudes are regions of high barometric pressure with calm and light winds and the Polar regions contain cold dense air that sinks to the earth's surface

Winds caused by local temperature changes include sea breezes, and land breezes.

Sea breezes are caused by the unequal heating of the land and an adjacent, large body of water. Land heats up faster than water. The movement of cool ocean air toward the land is called a sea breeze. Sea breezes usually begin blowing about mid-morning; ending about sunset.

A breeze that blows from the land to the ocean or a large lake is called a **land breeze.**

Monsoons are huge wind systems that cover large geographic areas and that reverse direction seasonally. The monsoons of India and Asia are examples of these seasonal winds. They alternate wet and dry seasons. As denser cooler air over the ocean moves inland, a steady seasonal wind called a summer or wet monsoon is produced.

Cloud types

Cirrus clouds - White and feathery high in sky

Cumulus – thick, white, fluffy

Stratus – layers of clouds cover most of the sky

Nimbus – heavy, dark clouds that represent thunderstorm clouds

Variation on the clouds mentioned above.

Cumulo-nimbus

Strato-nimbus

The air temperature at which water vapor begins to condense is called the **dew point.**

Relative humidity is the actual amount of water vapor in a certain volume of air compared to the maximum amount of water vapor this air could hold at a given temperature.

Knowledge of types of storms

A **thunderstorm** is a brief, local storm produced by the rapid upward movement of warm, moist air within a cumulo-nimbus cloud. Thunderstorms always produce lightning and thunder, accompanied by strong wind gusts and heavy rain or hail.

A severe storm with swirling winds that may reach speeds of hundreds of km per hour is called a **tornado**. Such a storm is also referred to as a "twister". The sky is covered by large cumulo-nimbus clouds and violent thunderstorms; a funnel-shaped swirling cloud may extend downward from a cumulonimbus cloud and reach the ground. Tornadoes are narrow storms that leave a narrow path of destruction on the ground.

A swirling, funnel-shaped cloud that **extends** downward and touches a body of water is called a **waterspout.**

Hurricanes are storms that develop when warm, moist air carried by trade winds rotates around a low-pressure "eye". A large, rotating, low-pressure system accompanied by heavy precipitation and strong winds is called a tropical cyclone or is better known as a hurricane. In the Pacific region, a hurricane is called a typhoon.

Storms that occur only in the winter are known as blizzards or ice storms. A **blizzard** is a storm with strong winds, blowing snow and frigid temperatures. An **ice storm** consists of falling rain that freezes when it strikes the ground, covering everything with a layer of ice.

SKILL 3.19 Identify the relationship between climate and landforms in both current and geologic time periods.

Tropical rain forests covered much of the world millions of years ago. Climatic changes currently limit this biome to about six percent of the Earth's land surface. Rain forests are found in South America, Africa, New Guinea, Malaysia, Burma, and Indonesia. The moist conditions and constant heat provide for a great growing environment. Fifty percent of all the species in the world are found in the rain forest. Only about one percent of the available sunlight reaches the forest floor. The climate is hot and humid; therefore the landform is a jungle. You would rule out polar region, too hot for trees and grasslands, too moist for a desert.

Desert biome – Hot like the rainforest but relatively little moisture. Sand accounts for 15 percent of desert terrain. Most deserts are bare rock or pebbles and gravel areas. The landform requires no moisture.

Tundra – Geologic time of the Ice Age has reports of a small number of mankind living there at the poles. The Indians, Aleuts, and Eskimos had little effect on the tundra's ecosystem. The climate is extremely cold. Therefore moss and lichens exist in this fragile environment of polar ice. More and more scientists are fearful that the polar caps are melting, which not only would change the landform and vegetation at the poles but also shift the water levels worldwide.

Taiga – Mild climate that is neither extremely hot nor cold has a hardy type of lumber such as birch, aspen, poplars, and willows. In the niche created by the cool shade of the large trees, there are a great variety of plants. They include lots of mosses, lichens, and ferns. The landform is often laced with rivers and streams. The soils of the taiga thaw out completely each summer and are the home to lots of tiny invertebrates and vertebrates. These microscopic organisms help break down the leaves and evergreen needles on the forest floor, enriching the soil. The recycled nutrients are then available for use by the taiga's trees to continue growing and producing for yet another season.

Grasslands – Grasslands have different names in different parts of the world. In North America they are called prairies, in Asia, steppes, in Africa and Australia, savannas and on and on. Grasses have deep root systems. Therefore the climate would have to be mild to support it. For thousands of years the growth cycle of the grasslands has created very rich top soil. Farming has converted much of the grasslands into growing crops. Only 11% of the Earth is suitable for farming. Grasses are pollinated by wind. The animals of this region tend to be fast and have mottled colors to blend in with the dry grass.

SKILL 3.20 Identify the movement of water in the hydrologic cycle, including types of precipitation and forms and causes of condensation.

Water that falls to Earth in the form of rain and snow is called **precipitation.** Precipitation is part of a continuous process in which water at the Earth's surface evaporates, condenses into clouds, and returns to Earth. This process is termed the **water cycle**. The water located below the surface is called groundwater.

Altitude impacts upon climatic conditions are primarily temperature and precipitation related. As altitude increases, climatic conditions become increasingly drier and colder. Solar radiation becomes more severe as altitude increases while the effects of convection forces are minimized. Climatic changes as a function of latitude follows a similar pattern. (As a reference, latitude moves either north or south from the equator). The climate becomes colder and drier as the distance from the equator increases. Proximity to land or water masses produces climatic conditions based upon the available moisture. Dry and arid climates prevail where moisture is scarce; lush tropical climates can prevail where moisture is abundant. Climate, as described above, depends upon the specific combination of conditions making up an area environment. Man impacts all environments by producing pollutants in earth, air, and water. It follows then, that man is a major player in world climatic conditions.

SKILL 3.21 Identify ways in which earth and water interact (e.g., soil absorption, run-off, percolation, and sinkholes).

Knowledge of soil types and properties

Soils are composed of particles of sand, clay, various minerals, tiny living organisms, and humus, plus the decayed remains of plants and animals.

Soils are divided into three classes according to their texture. These classes are sandy soils, clay soils, and loamy soils.

Sandy soils are gritty and their particles do not bind together firmly. Sandy soils are porous; water passes through them rapidly. Therefore, sandy soils do not hold much water therefore has poor **absorption.**

Clay soils are smooth and greasy; their particles bind together firmly. Clay soils are moist and usually do not allow water to pass through easily. This type of soil has the lowest potential for **run off.**

Loamy soils feel somewhat like velvet and their particles clump together. Loamy soils are made up of sand, clay, and silt. Loamy soils hold water but some water can pass through. **Percolation** is best in this type of soil.

Sinkholes

A large feature formed by dissolved limestone, which is calcium carbonate, includes sinkholes, caves and caverns. **Sinkholes** are funnel-shaped depressions created by dissolved limestone. Many sinkholes started life as a limestone cavern. Erosion weakens the cavern roof causing it to collapse, forming a sinkhole.

Groundwater usually contains large amounts of dissolved minerals, especially if the water flows through limestone. As groundwater drips through the roof of a cave, gases dissolved in the water can escape into the air. A deposit of calcium carbonate is left behind. Stalactites are icicle-like structures of calcium carbonate that hang from the roofs of caves. Water that falls on a constant spot on the cave floor and evaporates leaving a deposit of calcium carbonate, builds a stalagmite.

SKILL 3.22   Identify natural and man-made methods of water storage (eg., aquifers and reservoirs).

Precipitation that soaks into the ground through small pores or openings becomes groundwater. Gravity causes groundwater to move through interconnected pored rock formations from higher to lower elevations. The upper surface of the zone saturated with groundwater is the water table. A swamp is an area where the water table is at the surface. Sometimes the land dips below the water table and these areas fill with water forming lakes, ponds or streams. Groundwater that flows out from underground onto the surface is called a spring.

Permeable rocks filled with water are called **aquifers**. When a layer of permeable rock is trapped between two layers of impermeable rock, an aquifer is formed. Groundwater fills the pore spaces in the permeable rock. Layers of limestone are common aquifers. Groundwater provides drinking water for 53 % of the population in the United States that gets collected in **reservoirs.**

SKILL 3.23 Identify current problems related to water resources.

Groundwater provides drinking water for 53% of the population in the United States. Much groundwater is clean enough to drink without any type of treatment. Impurities in the water are filtered out by the rocks and soil through which it flows. However, many groundwater sources are becoming contaminated. Septic tanks, broken pipes, agriculture fertilizers, garbage dumps, rainwater runoff, leaking underground tanks, all pollute groundwater. Toxic chemicals from farmland mix with groundwater. Removal of large volumes of groundwater can cause collapse of soil and rock underground, causing the ground to sink. Along shorelines, excessive depletion of underground water supplies allows the intrusion of salt water into the fresh water field. The groundwater supply becomes undrinkable.

SKILL 3.24 Identify causes and effects of pollutants (eg., oil spills, acid rain, radioactivity, and ozone).

Pollutants are impurities in air and water that may be harmful to life. Spills from barges carrying large quantities of oil pollute the fish and beaches.

All acids contain hydrogen. Acidic substances from factory and car exhaust dissolve in rain water forming **acid rain.** Acid rain forms predominantly from pollutant oxides in the air (usually nitrogen-based NO_x or sulfur-based SO_x), which become hydrated into their acids (nitric or sulfuric acid). When the rain falls into stone, the acids can react with metallic compounds and gradually wear the stone away.

Radioactivity is the breaking down of atomic nuclei by releasing particles or electromagnetic radiation. Radioactive nuclei give off radiation in the form of streams of particles or energy. Alpha particles are positively charged particles consisting of two protons and two neutrons. It is the slowest form of radiation. It can be stopped by paper! Beta particles are electrons. It is produced when a neutron in the nucleus breaks up into a proton and an electron. The proton remains inside the nucleus, increasing its atomic number by one. But the electron is given off. They can be stopped by aluminum. Gamma rays are electromagnetic waves with extremely short wavelengths. They have no mass. They have no charge so they are not deflected by an electric field. Gamma rays travel at the speed of light. It takes a thick block of lead to stop them. Uranium is the source of radiation and therefore is radioactive. Marie Curie discovered new elements called radium and polonium that actually give off more radiation than uranium.

The major concern with radioactivity is in the case of a nuclear disaster. Medical misuse is also a threat. Radioactivity ionizes the air it travels through. It is strong enough to kill cancer cells or dangerous enough to cause illness or even death. Gamma rays can penetrate the body and damage cells. Protective clothing is needed when working with gamma rays. Electricity from nuclear energy uses the fuel like uranium 235. The devastation of the Russian nuclear power plant disaster has evacuated entire regions as the damage to the land and food source will last for hundreds of years.

COMPETENCY 4.0 KNOWLEDGE OF LIFE SCIENCE

SKILL 4.1   Identify the properties of living organisms.

The organization of living systems builds on levels from small to increasingly more large and complex. All aspects, whether it be a cell or an ecosystem have the same requirements to sustain life. Life is organized from simple to complex in the following way:

Organelles make up **cells** which make up **tissues** which make up **organs**. Groups of organs make up **organ systems**. Organ systems work together to provide life for the **organism.**

SKILL 4.2   Distinguish between living and nonliving things.

Several characteristics have been described to identify living versus non-living substance.

1. **Living things are made of cells**; they grow, are capable of reproduction and respond to stimuli.

2. **Living things must adapt to environmental changes or perish.**

3. **Living things carry on metabolic processes.** They use and make energy.

SKILL 4.3   Identify variations in life forms resulting in adaptation to the environment.

Darwin defined the theory of Natural Selection in the mid-1800's. Through the study of finches on the Galapagos Islands, Darwin theorized that nature selects the traits that are advantageous to the organism. Those that do not possess the desirable trait die and do not pass on their genes. Those more fit to survive reproduce, thus increasing that gene in the population. Darwin listed four principles to define natural selection:

1. The individuals in a certain species vary from generation to generation.
2. Some of the variations are determined by the genetic makeup of the species.
3. More individuals are produced than will survive.
4. Some genes allow for better survival of an animal.

Causes of evolution - Certain factors increase the chances of variability in a population, thus leading to evolution. Items that increase variability include mutations, sexual reproduction, immigration, large population, and variation in geographic local. Items that decrease variation would be natural selection, emigration, small population, and random mating.

Sexual selection - Obviously the genes that happen to come together determine the makeup of the gene pool. Animals that use mating behaviors may be successful or unsuccessful. An animal that lacks attractive plumage or has a weak mating call will not attract the female, thereby eventually limiting that gene in the gene pool. Mechanical isolation, where sex organs do not fit the female, has an obvious disadvantage.

SKILL 4.4   Identify cell organelles and their functions

Parts of Eukaryotic Cells

1. Nucleus - The brain of the cell. The nucleus contains:

> **chromosomes**- DNA, RNA and proteins tightly coiled to conserve space while providing a large surface area.
> **chromatin** - loose structure of chromosomes. Chromosomes are called chromatin when the cell is not dividing.
> **nucleoli** - where ribosomes are made. These are seen as dark spots in the nucleus.
> **nuclear membrane** - contains pores which let RNA out of the nucleus. The nuclear membrane is continuous with the endoplasmic reticulum which allows the membrane to expand or shrink if needed.

2. Ribosomes - the site of protein synthesis. Ribosomes may be free floating in the cytoplasm or attached to the endoplasmic reticulum. There may be up to a half a million ribosomes in a cell, depending on how much protein is made by the cell.

3. Endoplasmic Reticulum - These are folded and provide a large surface area. They are the "roadway" of the cell and allow for transport of materials throughout and out of the cell. The lumen of the endoplasmic reticulum helps to keep materials out of the cytoplasm and headed in the right direction. The endoplasmic reticulum is capable of building new membrane material. There are two types:

> **Smooth Endoplasmic Reticulum** - contain no ribosomes on their surface.

> **Rough Endoplasmic Reticulum** - contain ribosomes on their surface. This form of ER is abundant in cells that make many proteins, like in the pancreas, which produces many digestive enzymes.

4. Golgi Complex or Golgi Apparatus - This is a stacked structure to increase surface area. The Golgi Complex functions to sort, modify and package molecules that are made in other parts of the cells. These molecules are either sent out of the cell or to other organelles within the cell.

5. Lysosomes - found mainly in animal cells. These contain digestive enzymes that break down food, substances not needed, viruses, damaged cell components and eventually the cell itself. It is believed that lysosomes are responsible for the aging process.

6. Mitochondria - large organelles that make ATP to supply energy to the cell. Muscle cells have many mitochondria because they use a great deal of energy. The folds inside the mitochondria are called cristae. They provide a large surface area for the reactions of cellular respiration to occur. Mitochondria have their own DNA and are capable of reproducing themselves if a greater demand is made for additional energy. Mitochondria are found only in animal cells.

7. Plastids - found in photosynthetic organisms only. They are similar to the mitochondria due to the double membrane structure. They also have their own DNA and can reproduce if the need for the increased capture of sunlight becomes necessary. There are several types of plastids:

Chloroplasts - green, function in photosynthesis. They are capable of trapping sunlight.
Chromoplasts - make and store yellow and orange pigments; they provide color to leaves, flowers and fruits.
Amyloplasts - store starch and are used as a food reserve. They are abundant in roots like potatoes.

8. Cell Wall - found in plant cells only, it is composed of cellulose and fibers. It is thick enough for support and protection, yet porous enough to allow water and dissolved substances to enter. Cell walls are cemented to each other.

9. Vacuoles - hold stored food and pigments. Vacuoles are very large in plants. This is allows them to fill with water in order to provide turgor pressure. Lack of turgor pressure causes a plant to wilt.

10. Cytoskeleton - composed of protein filaments attached to the plasma membrane and organelles. They provide a framework for the cell and aid in cell movement. They constantly change shape and move about. Three types of fibers make up the cytoskeleton:

Microtubules - largest of the three makes up cilia and flagella for locomotion. Flagella grow from a basal body. Some examples are sperm cells, and tracheal cilia. Centrioles are also composed of microtubules. They form the spindle fibers that pull the cell apart into two cells during cell division. Centrioles are not found in the cells of higher plants.

Intermediate Filaments - they are smaller than microtubules but larger than microfilaments. They help the cell to keep its shape.

Microfilaments - smallest of the three, they are made of actin and small amounts of myosin (like in muscle cells). They function in cell movement like cytoplasmic streaming, endocytosis and ameboid movement. This structure pinches the two cells apart after cell division, forming two cells.

SKILL 4.5   Identify the sequence of events in mitosis and meiosis and the significance of each process.

The purpose of cell division is to provide growth and repair in body (somatic) cells and to replenish or create sex cells for reproduction. There are two forms of cell division. Mitosis is the division of somatic cells and **meiosis** is the division of sex cells (eggs and sperm). The table below summarizes the major differences between the two processes.

<table>
<tr><td>

MITOSIS

1. Division of somatic cell
2. Two cells result from each division

3. Chromosome number is identical to parent cells.
4. For cell growth and repair

</td><td>

MEIOSIS

1. Division of sex cells
2. Four cells or polar bodies result from each division

3. Chromosome number is half the number of parent cells
4. Recombinations provide genetic diversity

</td></tr>
</table>

Some terms to know:

gamete - sex cell or germ cell; eggs and sperm.
chromatin - loose chromosomes; this state is found when the cell is not dividing.
chromosome - tightly coiled, visible chromatin; this state is found when the cell is dividing.
homologues - chromosomes that contain the same information. They are of the same length and contain the same genes.
diploid - 2n number; diploid chromosomes are a pair of chromosomes (somatic cells).
haploid - 1n number; haploid chromosomes are a half of a pair (sex cells).

MITOSIS

The cell cycle is the life cycle of the cell. It is divided into two stages; **Interphase** and the **mitotic division** where the cell is actively dividing. Interphase is divided into three steps; G1 (growth) period, where the cell is growing and metabolizing, S period (synthesis) where new DNA and enzymes are being made and the G2 phase (growth) where new proteins and organelles are being made to prepare for cell division. The mitotic stage consists of the stages of mitosis and the division of the cytoplasm.

GENERAL SCIENCE

The stages of mitosis and their events are as follows. Be sure to know the correct order of steps. (IPMAT)

1. Interphase - chromatin is loose, chromosomes are replicated, cell metabolism is occurring. Interphase is technically <u>not</u> a stage of mitosis

2. Prophase - once the cell enters prophase, it proceeds through the following steps continuously, with no stopping. The chromatin condenses to become visible chromosomes. The nucleolus disappears and the nuclear membrane breaks apart. Mitotic spindles form which will eventually pull the chromosomes apart. They are composed of microtubules. The cytoskeleton breaks down and the spindles are pushed to the poles or opposite ends of the cell by the action of centrioles.

3. Metaphase - kinetechore fibers attach to the chromosomes which causes the chromosomes to line up in the center of the cell (think **m**iddle for **m**etaphase)

4. Anaphase - centromeres split in half and homologous chromosomes separate. The chromosomes are pulled to the poles of the cell, with identical sets at either end.

5. Telophase - two nuclei for with a full set of DNA that is identical to the parent cell. The nucleoli become visible and the nuclear membrane reassembles. A cell plate is visible in plant cells, whereas a cleavage furrow is formed in animal cells. The cell is pinched into two cells. Cytokinesis, or division, of the cytoplasm and organelles occurs.

Meiosis contains the same five stages as mitosis, but is repeated in order to reduce the chromosome number by one half. This way, when the sperm and egg join during fertilization, the haploid number is reached. The steps of meiosis are as follows:

Major function of Meiosis I - chromosomes are replicated; cells remain diploid.

Prophase I - replicated chromosomes condense and pair with homologues. This forms a tetrad. Crossing over (the exchange of genetic material between homologues to further increase diversity) occurs during Prophase I.
Metaphase I - homologous sets attach to spindle fibers after lining up in the middle of the cell.
Anaphase I - sister chromatids remain joined and move to the poles of the cell.
Telophase I - two new cells are formed, chromosome number is still diploid

Major function of Meiosis II - to reduce the chromosome number in half.

Prophase II - chromosomes condense.
Metaphase II - spindle fibers form again, sister chromatids line up in center of cell, centromeres divide and sister chromatids separate.
Anaphase II - separated chromosomes move to opposite ends of cell.
Telophase II - four haploid cells form for each original sperm germ cell. One viable egg cell gets all the genetic information and three polar bodies form with no DNA. The nuclear membrane reforms and cytokinesis occurs.

SKILL 4.6   Identify the consequences of irregularities or interruptions of mitosis and meiosis.

Since it's not a perfect world, mistakes happen. Inheritable changes in DNA are called **mutations**. Mutations may be errors in replication or a spontaneous rearrangement of one or more segments by factors like radioactivity, drugs, or chemicals. The amount of the change is not as critical as where the change is. Mutations may occur on somatic or sex cells. Usually the ones on sex cells are more dangerous since they contain the basis of all information for the developing offspring. Mutations are not always bad. They are the basis of evolution, and if they make a more favorable variation that enhances the organism's survival, then they are beneficial. But, mutations may also lead to abnormalities, birth defects, and even death. There are several types of mutations; let's suppose a normal sequence was as follows:

Normal: A B C D E F

Duplication - one gene is repeated.   A B C C D E F

Inversion - a segment of the sequence is flipped around. A E D C B F

Deletion - a gene is left out.   A B C E F

Insertion or Translocation - a segment from another place on the DNA is stuck in the wrong place.   A B C R S D E F

Breakage - a piece is lost.   A B C (DEF is lost)

Nondisjunction - during meiosis, chromosomes fail to separate properly. One sex cell may get both genes and another may get none. Depending on the chromosomes involved this may or may not be serious. Offspring end up with either an extra chromosome or are missing one. An example of nondisjunction is Down Syndrome, where three #21 chromosomes are present.

SKILL 4.7   Identify cell types, structures and functions.

Animal cells – begin a discussion of the nucleus as a round body inside the cell. It controls the cell's activities. The nuclear membrane contains threadlike structures called chromosomes. The genes are units that control cell activities found in the nucleus. The cytoplasm has many structures in it. Vacuoles contain the food for the cell. Other vacuoles contain waste materials. Animal cells differ from plant cells because they have cell membranes.

Plant cells – have cell walls. A cell wall differs from cell membranes. The cell membrane is very thin and is a part of the cell. The cell wall is thick and is a nonliving part of the cell. Chloroplasts are other structures not found in animals. They are little bundles of chlorophyll. The structure of the cell is often related to the cell's function. Root hair cells differ from flower stamens or leaf epidermal cells. They all have different functions.

Single cells – A single cell organism is called a **protist.** When you look under a microscope the animal-like protists are called **protozoans.** They do not have chloroplasts. They are usually classified by the way they move for food. Amoebas engulf other protists by flowing around and over them. The paramecium has a hair like structure allows it to move back and forth like tiny oars searching for food. The euglena is an example of a protozoan that moves with a tail-like structure called flagella.

Plant-like protists have cell walls and float in the ocean. **Bacteria** are the simplest protists. A bacterial cell is surrounded by a cell wall, but there is no nucleus inside the cell. Most bacteria do not contain chlorophyll so they do not make their own food. The classification of bacteria is by shape. Cocci are round, bacilli are rod-shaped, and spirilla are spiral shaped.

SKILL 4.8   Apply principles of Mendelian genetics in working monohybrid and dihybrid crosses and crosses involving linked genes.

Gregor Mendel is recognized as the father of genetics. His work in the late 1800's is the basis of our knowledge of genetics. Although unaware of the presence of DNA or genes, Mendel realized there were factors (now known as genes) that were transferred from parents to their offspring. Mendel worked with pea plants and fertilized the plants himself, keeping track of subsequent generations which led to the Mendelian laws of genetics. Mendel found that two "factors" governed each trait, one from each parent. Traits or characteristics came in several forms, known as alleles. For example, the trait of flower color had white alleles and purple alleles. Mendel formed three laws:

> **Law of dominance** - in a pair of alleles, one trait may cover up the allele of the other trait. Example: brown eyes are dominant to blue eyes.

> **Law of segregation** - only one of the two possible alleles from each parent is passed on to the offspring from each parent. (During meiosis, the haploid number insures that half the sex cells get one allele, half get the other).

> **Law of independent assortment** - alleles sort independently of each other. (Many combinations are possible depending on which sperm ends up with which egg. Compare this to the many combinations of hands possible when dealing a deck of cards).

> **monohybrid cross** - a cross using only one trait.

> **dihybrid cross** - a cross using two traits. More combinations are possible.

Punnet squares - these are used to show the possible ways that genes combine or probability of the occurrence of a certain genotype or phenotype. One parent's genes are put at the top of the box and the other parent at the side of the box. Genes combine on the square just like numbers that are added in addition tables we learned in elementary school.

Example: Monohybrid Cross - four possible gene combinations

Example: Dihybrid Cross - sixteen possible gene combinations

SKILL 4.9 **Apply principles of human genetics, including relationships between genotypes and phenotypes and causes and effects of disorders.**

SOME DEFINITIONS TO KNOW -

Dominant - the stronger of the two traits. If a dominant gene is present, it will be expressed. Shown by a capital letter.

Recessive - the weaker of the two traits. In order for the recessive gene to be expressed, there must be two recessive genes present. Shown by a lower case letter.

Homozygous - (purebred) having two of the same genes present; an organism may be homozygous dominant with two dominant genes or homozygous recessive with two recessive genes.

Heterozygous - (hybrid) having one dominant gene and one recessive gene. The dominant gene will be expressed due to the Law of Dominance.

Genotype - the genes the organism has. Genes are represented with letters. AA, Bb, and tt are examples of genotypes.

Phenotype - how the trait is expressed in an organism. Blue eyes, brown hair, and red flowers are examples of phenotypes.

Incomplete dominance - neither gene masks the other; a new phenotype is formed. For example, red flowers and white flowers may have equal strength. A heterozygote (Rr) would have pink flowers. If a problem occurs with a third phenotype, incomplete dominance is occurring.

Codominance - genes may form new phenotypes. The ABO blood grouping is an example of co-dominance. A and B are of equal strength and O is recessive. Therefore, type A blood may have the genotypes of AA or AO, type B blood may have the genotypes of BB or BO, type AB blood has the genotype A and B, and type O blood has two recessive O genes.

Linkage - genes that are found on the same chromosome usually appear together unless crossing over has occurred in meiosis. (Example - blue eyes and blonde hair)

Lethal alleles - these are usually recessive due to the early death of the offspring. If a 2:1 ratio of alleles is found in offspring, a lethal gene combination is usually the reason. Some examples of lethal alleles include sickle cell anemia, tay-sachs and cystic fibrosis. Usually the coding for an important protein is affected.

Inborn errors of metabolism - these occur when the protein affected is an enzyme. Examples include PKU (phenylketonuria) and albanism.

Polygenic characters - many alleles code for a phenotype. There may be as many as twenty genes that code for skin color. This is why there is such a variety of skin tones. Another example is height. A couple of medium height may have very tall offspring.

Sex linked traits - the Y chromosome found only in males (XY) carries very little genetic information, whereas the X chromosome found in females (XX) carries very important information. Since men have no second X chromosome to cover up a recessive gene, the recessive trait is expressed more often in men. Women need the recessive gene on both X chromosomes to show the trait. Examples of sex linked traits include hemophilia and color-blindness.

Sex influenced traits - traits are influenced by the sex hormones. Male pattern baldness is an example of a sex influenced trait. Testosterone influences the expression of the gene. Mostly men loose their hair due to this.

SKILL 4.10   Identify the role of DNA and RNA in protein synthesis, translation, transcription, and replication.

DNA and DNA REPLICATION

The modern definition of a gene is that of a unit of genetic information. DNA makes up genes which in turn make up the chromosomes. DNA is wound tightly around proteins in order to conserve space. The DNA/protein combination makes up the chromosome. DNA controls the synthesis of proteins, thereby controlling the total cell activity. DNA is capable of making copies of itself.

To review the structure of DNA:

1. Made of nucleotides; a five carbon sugar, phosphate group and nitrogen base (either adenine, guanine, cytosine or thymine).

2. Consist of a sugar/phosphate backbone which is covalently bonded. The bases are joined down the center of the molecule and are attached by hydrogen bonds which are easily broken during replication.

3. The amount of adenine equals the amount of thymine and cytosine equals the amount of guanine.

4. The shape is that of a twisted ladder called a double helix. The sugar/phosphates make up the sides of the ladder and the base pairs make up the rungs of the ladder.

DNA Replication

Enzymes control each step of the replication of DNA. The molecule untwists. The hydrogen bonds between the bases break and serve as a pattern for replication. Free nucleotides found inside the nucleus join on to form a new strand. Two new pieces of DNA are formed which are identical. This is a very accurate process. There is only one mistake for every billion nucleotides added. This is because there are enzymes (polymerases) present that proofread the molecule. In eukaryotes, replication occurs in many places along the DNA at once. The molecule may open up at many places like a broken zipper. In prokaryotic circular plasmids, replication begins at a point on the plasmid and goes in both directions until it meets itself.

Base pairing rules are important in determining a new strand of DNA sequence. For example say our original strand of DNA had the sequence as follows:

1. A T C G G C A A T A G C   This may be called our sense strand as it contains a sequence that makes sense or codes for something. The complementary strand (or other side of the ladder) would follow base pairing rules (A bonds with T and C bonds with G and would read:

2. T A G C C G T T A T C G   When the molecule opens up and nucleotides join on, the base pairing rules create two new identical strands of DNA

1. A T C G G C A A T A G C   and   A T C G G C A A T A G C
   T A G C C G T T A T C G   2. T A G C C G T T A T C G

Protein Synthesis

It is necessary for cells to manufacture new proteins for growth and repair of the organism. Protein Synthesis is the process that allows the DNA code to be read and carried out of the nucleus into the cytoplasm in the form of RNA. This is where the ribosomes are found, which are the sites of protein synthesis. The protein is then assembled according to the instructions on the DNA. There are several types of RNA. Familiarize yourself with where they are found and their function.

Messenger RNA - (mRNA) copies the code from DNA in the nucleus and takes it to the ribosomes in the cytoplasm.

Transfer RNA - (tRNA) free floating in the cytoplasm. Its job is to carry and position amino acids for assembly on the ribosome.

Ribosomal RNA - (rRNA) found in the ribosomes. They make a place for the proteins to be made. Much research is being done currently on rRNA and it is believed to have many important functions.

Along with enzymes and amino acids, the RNA's function to assist in the building of proteins. There are two stages of protein synthesis:

Transcription - basically, this phase allows for the assembly of mRNA and occurs in the nucleus where the DNA is found. The DNA splits open and the mRNA reads the code and "transcribes" the sequence onto a single strand of mRNA. For example, if the code on the DNA is: T A C C T C G T A C G A , the mRNA will make a complementary strand reading: A U G G A G C A U G C U (Remember that uracil replaces thymine in RNA.) Each group of three bases is called a **codon**. The codon will eventually code for a specific amino acid to be carried to the ribosome. "Start" codons begin the building of the protein and "stop" codons end transcription. When the stop codon is reached, the mRNA separates from the DNA and leaves the nucleus for the cytoplasm.

Translation - basically, this is the assembly of the amino acids to build the protein and occurs in the cytoplasm. The nucleotide sequence is translated to choose the correct amino acid sequence. As the rRNA translates the code at the ribosome, tRNA's which contain an **anticodon** seek out the correct amino acid and bring it back to the ribosome. For example, using the codon sequence from the example above:

the mRNA reads A U G / G A G / C A U / G C U
the anticodons are UA C / C U C / G U A / C G A (which you would be given and are not expected to memorize) the amino acid sequence would be:

Methionine (start) - Glu - His - Ala. Be sure to note if the table you are given is written according to the codon sequence or the anticodon sequence. It will be specified.

This whole process is accomplished through the assistance of **activating enzymes**. Each of the twenty amino acids has their own enzyme. The enzyme binds the amino acid to the tRNA. When the amino acids get close to each other on the ribosome, they bond together using peptide bonds. The start and stop codons are called nonsense codons. There is one start codon (AUG) and three stop codons. (UAA, UGA and UAG) Addition mutations will cause the whole code to shift, thereby producing the wrong protein or at times, no protein at all.

SKILL 4.11   Distinguish between prokaryotes and eukaryotes.

The cell is the basic unit of all living things. There are two types of cells. **Prokaryotic** cells consist only of bacteria and blue-green algae. Bacteria were most likely the first cells and date back in the fossil record to 3.5 billion years ago The important things that put these cells in their own group are:

1. They have no defined nucleus or nuclear membrane. The DNA and ribosomes float freely within the cell.

2. They have a thick cell wall. This is for protection, to give shape and to keep the cell from bursting.

3. The cell walls contain amino sugars (glycoproteins). Penicillin works by disrupting the cell wall, which is bad for the bacteria, but will not harm the host.

4. Some have a capsule made of polysaccharides which make the bacteria sticky (like on your teeth).

5. Some have pili, which is a protein strand. This also allows for attachment of the bacteria and may be used for sexual reproduction called conjugation.

6. Some have flagella for movement.

Eukaryotic cells are found in protists, fungi, plants and animals. Some features of eukaryotic cells include:

1. They are usually larger than prokaryotic cells.

2. They contain many organelles, which are membrane bound areas for specific cell functions.

3. They contain a cytoskeleton which provides a protein framework for the cell.

4. They contain cytoplasm to support the organelles and contain the ions and molecules necessary for cell function.

SKILL 4.12   Taxonomy and classification of bacteria, protists, and fungi.

Carolus Linnaeus is termed the father of taxonomy. **Taxonomy** is the science of classification. Linnaeus based his system on morphology (study of structure). Later on, evolutionary relationships (phylogeny) were also used to sort and group species. The modern classification system uses binomial nomenclature. This consists of a two word name for every species. The genus is the first part of the name and the species is the second part. Notice in the levels explained below that Homo sapiens is the scientific name for humans. Starting with the kingdom, the groups get smaller and more alike as one moves down the levels in the classification of humans:

Kingdom: Animalia, **Phylum:** Chordata, **Subphylum:** Vertebrata, **Class:** Mammalia, **Order:** Primate, **Family:** Hominidae, **Genus:** Homo, **Species:** sapiens

Species are defined by the ability to successfully reproduce with members of their own kind.

Kingdom Monera - bacteria and blue-green algae, prokaryotic, having no true nucleus, unicellular.

Kingdom Protista - eukaryotic, unicellular, some are photosynthetic, some are consumers.

Kingdom Fungi - eukaryotic, multicellular, absorptive consumers, contain a chitin cell wall.

Bacteria are classified according to their morphology (shape). **Bacilli** are rod shaped bacteria **coccus** are round bacteria and **spirillum** are spiral shaped. The **gram stain** is a staining procedure used to identify bacteria. Gram positive bacteria pick up the stain and turn purple. Gram negative bacteria do not pick up the stain and are pink in color. Microbiologists use methods of locomotion, reproduction, and how the organism obtains its food to classify protista.

Methods of locomotion - Flagellates have a flagellum, ciliates have cilia and ameboids move through use of pseudopodia.

Methods of reproduction - binary fission is simply dividing in half and is asexual. All new organisms are exact clones of the parent. Sexual modes provide more diversity. Bacteria can reproduce sexually through conjugation, where genetic material is exchanged.

Methods of obtaining nutrition - photosynthetic organisms or producers, convert sunlight to chemical energy, consumers or heterotrophs eat other living things. Saprophytes are consumers that live off dead or decaying material.

SKILL 4.13 Identify helpful and harmful interactions between microbes and humans.

Although bacteria and fungi may cause disease, they are also beneficial for use as medicines and food. Penicillin is derived from a fungus that is capable of destroying the cell wall of bacteria. Most antibiotics work in this way. Viral diseases have been fought through the use of vaccination, where a small amount of the virus is introduced so the immune system is able to recognize it upon later infection. Antibodies are more quickly manufactured when the host has had prior exposure. Viruses are difficult to treat because antibiotics are ineffective against them. That is why doctors do not usually prescribe antibiotics for those who have a cold or the flu—common viral infections.

SKILL 4.14 Identify the structures and functions of the parts of various types of plants.

Plant Tissues - specialization of tissue enabled plants to get larger. Be familiar with the following tissues and their functions.

Xylem - transports water.

Phloem - transports food (glucose).

Cortex - storage of food and water.

Epidermis – protection.

Endodermis - controls movement between the cortex and the cell interior.

Pericycle - meristematic tissue which can divide when necessary.

Pith - storage in stems.

Sclerenchyma and collenchyma - support in stems.

Stomata - openings on the underside of leaves. They let carbon dioxide in and water out (transpiration).

Guard cells - control the size of the stomata. If the plant has to conserve water, the stomates will close.

Palisade mesophyll - contain chloroplasts in leaves. Site of photosynthesis.

Spongy mesophyll - open spaces in the leaf that allows for gas circulation.

Seed coat - protective covering on a seed.

Cotyledon - small seed leaf that emerges when the seed germinates.

Endosperm - food supply in the seed.

Apical meristem - this is an area of cell division allowing for growth.

Flowers are the reproductive organs of the plant. Know the following functions and locations:

Pedicel - supports the weight of the flower.

Receptacle - holds the floral organs at the base of the flower.

Sepals - green leaflike parts that cover the flower prior to blooming.

Petals - contain coloration by pigments to attract insects to assist in pollination.

Anther - male part that produces pollen.

Filament - supports the anther; the filament and anther make up the stamen.

Stigma - female part that holds pollen grains that came from the male part.

Style - tube that leads to the ovary (female).

Ovary - contains the ovules; the stigma, style and ovary make up the carpel.

SKILL 4.15 Identify the major steps of the plant physiological processes of photosynthesis, transpiration, reproduction and respiration.

Photosynthesis is the process by which plants make carbohydrates from the energy of the sun, carbon dioxide and water. Oxygen is a waste product. Photosynthesis occurs in the chloroplast where the pigment chlorophyll traps sun energy. It is divided into two major steps:

> **Light Reactions** - Sunlight is trapped, water is split, and oxygen is given off. ATP is made and hydrogens reduce NADP to $NADPH_2$. The light reactions occur in light. The products of the light reactions enter into the dark reactions (Calvin cycle).

> **Dark Reactions** - Carbon dioxide enters during the dark reactions which can occur with or without the presence of light. The energy transferred from $NADPH_2$ and ATP allow for the fixation of carbon into glucose.

> **Respiration** - during times of decreased light, plants break down the products of photosynthesis through cellular respiration. Glucose, with the help of oxygen breaks down and produces carbon dioxide and water as wastes. Approximately fifty percent of the products of photosynthesis are used by the plant for energy.

> **Transpiration** - water travels up the xylem of the plant through the process of transpiration. Water sticks to itself (cohesion) and to the walls of the xylem (adhesion). As it evaporates through the stomata of the leaves, the water is pulled up the column from the roots. Environmental factors such as heat and wind increase the rate of transpiration. High humidity will decrease the rate of transpiration.

Reproduction - Angiosperms are the largest group in the plant kingdom. They are the flowering plants and produce true seeds for reproduction. They arose about seventy million years ago when the dinosaurs were disappearing. The land was drying up and their ability to produce seeds that could remain dormant until conditions became acceptable and allowed for their success. They also had more advanced vascular tissue and larger leaves for increased photosynthesis. Angiosperms reproduce through a method of **double fertilization**. An ovum is fertilized by two sperm. One sperm produces they new plant, the other forms the food supply for the developing plant.

Seed dispersal - success of plant reproduction involves the seed moving away from the parent plant to decrease competition for space, water and minerals. Seeds may be carried by wind (maples), water (palms), carried by animals (burrs) or ingested by animals and released in their feces in another area.

GENERAL SCIENCE

SKILL 4.16 Classify the major groups of plants.

NONVASCULAR PLANTS - small in size, did not require vascular tissue (xylem and phloem) as individual cells were close to their environment. The nonvascular plants have no true leaves, stems or roots.

Division Bryophyta - mosses and liverworts, these plants have a dominant gametophyte generation. They possess rhizoids, which are root like structures. Moisture in their environment is required for reproduction and absorption.

VASCULAR PLANTS - the development of vascular tissue enabled these plants to grow in size. Xylem and phloem allowed for the transport of water and minerals up to the top of the plant and food manufactured in the leaves to the bottom of the plant. All vascular plants have a dominant sporophyte generation.

Division Lycophyta - club mosses; these plants reproduce with spores and require water for reproduction.

Division Sphenophyta - horsetails; also reproduce with spores. These plants have small, needle-like leaves and rhizoids. Require moisture for reproduction.

Division Pterophyta - ferns; reproduce with spores and flagellated sperm. These plants have true stem and need moisture for reproduction.

Gymnosperms - The word means "naked seed". These were the first plants to evolve with the use of seeds for reproduction which made them less dependent on water to assist in reproduction. Their seeds could travel by wind. Pollen from the male was also easily carried by the wind. Gymnosperms have cones which protect the seeds.

Division Cycadophyta - cycads; these plants look like palms with cones.

Divison Ghetophyta - desert dwellers.

Division Coniferophyta - pines; these plants have needles and cones.

Divison Ginkgophyta - the Ginkgo is the only member of this division.

Angiosperms (Division Anthophyta) - Angiosperms are the largest group in the plant kingdom. They are the flowering plants and produce true seeds for reproduction.

SKILL 4.17 Identify the structures and functions of the organs and systems of various kinds of animals.

Skeletal System - The skeletal system functions in support. Vertebrates have an endoskeleton, with muscles attached to bones. Skeletal proportions are controlled by area to volume relationships. Body size and shape is limited due to the forces of gravity. Surface area is increased to improve efficiency in all organ systems.

Muscular System - function is for movement. There are three types of muscle tissue. Skeletal muscle is voluntary. These muscles are attached to bones. Smooth muscle is involuntary. It is found in organs and enable functions such as digestion and respiration. Cardiac muscle is a specialized type of smooth muscle.

Nervous System - The neuron is the basic unit of the nervous system. It consists of an axon, which carries impulses away from the cell body, the dendrite, which carries impulses toward the cell body and the cell body, which contains the nucleus. Synapses are spaces between neurons. Chemicals called neurotransmitters are found close to the synapse. The myelin sheath, composed of Schwann cells cover the neurons and provide insulation.

Digestive System - The function of the digestive system is to break down food and absorb it into the blood stream where it can be delivered to all cells of the body for use in cellular respiration. As animals evolved, digestive systems changed from simple absorption to a system with a separate mouth and anus, capable of allowing the animal to become independent of a host.

Respiratory System - This system functions in the gas exchange of needed oxygen and carbon dioxide waste. It delivers oxygen to the bloodstream and picks up carbon dioxide for release out of the body. Simple animals diffuse gases from and to their environment. Gills allowed aquatic animals to exchange gases in a fluid medium by removing dissolved oxygen from the water. Lungs maintained a fluid environment for gas exchange in terrestrial animals.

Circulatory System - The function of the circulatory system is to carry oxygenated blood and nutrients to all cells of the body and return carbon dioxide waste to be expelled from the lungs. Animals evolved from an open system to a closed system with vessels leading to and from the heart.

SKILL 4.18   Identify the major steps of the physiological process in animals, such as respiration, reproduction, digestion and circulation.

Section 4.23 overlaps with other animals that are mammals.

Animal respiration takes in oxygen and gives off waste gases. For instance a fish uses its gills to extract oxygen from the water. Bubbles are evidence that waste gasses are expelled. Respiration without oxygen is called anaerobic respiration. Anaerobic respiration in animal cells is also called lactic acid fermentation. The end product is lactic acid.

Animal reproduction can be asexual or sexual. Geese lay eggs. Animals such as bear cubs, deer, and rabbits are born alive. Some animals reproduce frequently others do not. Some animals only produce one baby others produce many.

Animal digestion – some animals only eat meat while others only eat plants. Many animals do both. Nature has created animals with structural adaptations so they may obtain food through sharp teeth or long facial structures. Digestion's purpose is to break down carbohydrates, fats and proteins. Many organs are needed to digest food starting with the mouth. Certain animals such as birds have beaks to puncture wood or allow for large fish to be consumed. The tooth structure of a beaver is designed to cut down trees. Tigers are known for their sharp teeth used to rip hides from their prey. Enzymes are catalysts that help speed up chemical reactions by lowering effective activation energy. Enzyme rate is affected by temperature, pH, and the amount of substrate. Saliva is an enzyme that changes starches into sugars.

Animal circulation – The blood temperature of all mammals stays constant regardless of the outside temperature (within reason). This is called warm-blooded, while cold-blooded animals circulation will vary with the temperature.

SKILL 4.19 Identify patterns of animal behavior.

Behavior - animal behavior is responsible for courtship leading to mating, communication between species, territoriality and aggression between animals and dominance within a group. Behaviors may include body posture, mating calls, display of feathers or fur, coloration or bearing of teeth and claws.

Innate behavior - behaviors that are inborn or instinctual. An environmental stimulus such as the length of day or temperature results in a behavior. Hibernation among some animals is an innate behavior.

Learned behavior - behavior that is modified due to past experience is called learned behavior.

SKILL 4.20   Classify the major groups of animals.

Annelida - the segmented worms; the first with specialized tissue. The circulatory system is more advanced in these worms and is a closed system with blood vessels. The nephridia are their excretory organs. They are hermaphrodidic and each worm fertilizes the other upon mating. They support themselves with a hydrostatic skeleton and have circular and longitudinal muscles for movement.

Mollusca - clams, octopus; the soft bodied animals. These animals have a muscular foot for movement. They breathe through gills and most are able to make a shell for protection from predators. They have an open circulatory system, with sinuses bathing the body regions.

Arthropoda - insects, crustaceans and spiders; this is the largest group of the animal kingdom. Phylum arthropoda accounts for about 85% of all the animal species. Animals in the arthropoda phylum possess an exoskeleton made of chitin. They must molt to grow. Insects, for example, go through four stages of development. They begin as an egg, hatches into a larva, forms a pupa, then emerges as an adult. Arthropods breathe through gills, trachae or book lungs. Movement varies, with members being able to swim, fly and crawl. There is a division of labor among the appendages (legs, antennae, etc). This is an extremely successful phylum, with members occupying diverse habitats.

Echinodermata - sea urchins and starfish; these animals have spiny skin. Their habitat is marine. They have tube feet for locomotion and feeding.

Chordata - all animals with a notocord or a backbone. The classes in this phylum include Agnatha (jawless fish), Chondrichthyes (cartilage fish), Osteichthyes (bony fish), Amphibia (frogs and toads; gills which are replaced by lungs during development), Reptilia (snakes, lizards; the first to lay eggs with a protective covering), Aves (birds; warm-blooded with wings consisting of a particular shape and composition designed for flight), and Mammalia (animals with body hair that bear their young alive, possess mammary glands that produce milk, and warm-blooded).

SKILL 4.21 **Identify the major characteristics and processes of world biomes and communities, including succession, energy flow in food chains and interrelationships of organisms.**

Ecology is the study of organisms, where they live and their interactions with the environment. A **population** is a group of the same species in a specific area. A **community** is a group of populations residing in the same area. Communities that are ecologically similar in regards to temperature, rainfall and the species that live there are called **biomes**. Specific biomes include:

Marine - covers 75% of the earth. This biome is organized by the depth of the water. The intertidal zone is from the tide line to the edge of the water. The littoral zone is from the waters edge to the open sea. It includes coral reef habitats and is the most densely populated area of the marine biome. The open sea zone is divided into the epipelagic zone and the pelagic zone. The epipelagic zone receives more sunlight and has a larger number of species. The ocean floor is called the benthic zone and is populated with bottom feeders.

Tropical Rain Forest - temperature is constant (25 degrees C), rainfall exceeds 200 cm. per year. Located around the area of the equator, the rain forest has abundant, diverse species of plants and animals.

Savanna - temperatures range from 0 - 25 degrees C depending on the location. Rainfall is from 90 to 150 cm per year. Plants include shrubs and grasses. The savanna is a transitional biome between the rain forest and the desert.

Desert - temperatures range from 10 - 38 degrees C. Rainfall is under 25 cm per year. Plant species include xerophytes and succulents. Lizards, snakes and small mammals are common animals.

Temperate Deciduous Forest - temperature ranges from -24 to 38 degrees C. Rainfall is between 65 to 150 cm per year. Deciduous trees are common, as well as deer, bear and squirrels.

Taiga - temperatures range from -24 to 22 degrees C. Rainfall is between 35 to 40 cm per year. Taiga is located very north and very south of the equator, getting close to the poles. Plant life includes conifers and plants that can withstand harsh winters. Animals include weasels, mink, and moose.

Tundra - temperatures range from -28 to 15 degrees C. Rainfall is limited, ranging from 10 to 15 cm per year. The tundra is located even further north and south of the taiga. Common plants include lichens and mosses. Animals include polar bears and musk ox.

GENERAL SCIENCE

Polar or Permafrost - temperature ranges from -40 to 0 degrees C. It rarely gets above freezing. Rainfall is below 10 cm per year. Most water is bound up as ice. Life is limited.

Succession - Succession is an orderly process of replacing a community that has been damaged or has begun where no life previously existed. Primary succession occurs after a community has been totally wiped out by a natural disaster or where life never existed before, as in a flooded area. Secondary succession takes place in communities that were once flourishing but disturbed by some source, either man or nature, but not totally stripped. A climax community is a community that is established and flourishing.

Definitions of feeding relationships:

Parasitism - two species that occupy a similar place; the parasite benefits from the relationship, the host is harmed.

Commensalism - two species that occupy a similar place; neither species is harmed or benefits from the relationship.

Mutualism (symbiosis)- two species that occupy a similar place; both species benefit from the relationship.

Competition - two species that occupy the same habitat or eat the same food are said to be in competition with each other.

Predation - animals that eat other animals are called predators. They animals they feed on are called the prey. Population growth depends upon competition for food, water, shelter and space. The amount of predators determines the amount of prey, which in turn affects the number of predators.

Carrying Capacity - this is the total amount of life a habitat can support. Once the habitat runs out of food, water, shelter or space, the carrying capacity decreases, and then stabilizes.

Biogeochemical cycles

Essential elements are recycled through an ecosystem. At times, the element needs to be "fixed" in a useable form. Cycles are dependent on plants, algae and bacteria to fix nutrients for use by animals.

Water cycle - 2% of all the available water is fixed and unavailable in ice or the bodies of organisms. Available water includes surface water (lakes, ocean, and rivers) and ground water (aquifers, wells) 96% of all available water is from ground water. Water is recycled through the processes of evaporation and precipitation. The water present now is the water that has been here since our atmosphere formed.

Carbon cycle - Ten percent of all available carbon in the air (from carbon dioxide gas) is fixed by photosynthesis. Plants fix carbon in the form of glucose, animals eat the plants and are able to obtain their source of carbon. When animals release carbon dioxide through respiration, the plants again have a source of carbon to fix again.

Nitrogen cycle - Eighty percent of the atmosphere is in the form of nitrogen gas. Nitrogen must be fixed and taken out of the gaseous form to be incorporated into an organism. Only a few genera of bacteria have the correct enzymes to break the triple bond between nitrogen atoms. These bacteria live within the roots of legumes (peas, beans, alfalfa) and add bacteria to the soil so it may be taken up by the plant. Nitrogen is necessary to make amino acids and the nitrogenous bases of DNA.

Phosphorus cycle - Phosphorus exists as a mineral and is not found in the atmosphere. Fungi and plant roots have a structure called mycorrhizae that are able to fix insoluble phosphates into useable phosphorus. Urine and decayed matter returns phosphorus to the earth where it can be fixed in the plant. Phosphorus is needed for the backbone of DNA and for ATP manufacture.

Ecological Problems - nonrenewable resources are fragile and must be conserved for use in the future. Man's impact and knowledge of conservation will control our future.

Biological magnification - chemicals and pesticides accumulate along the food chain. Tertiary consumers have more accumulated toxins than animals at the bottom of the food chain.

Simplification of the food web - Three major crops feed the world (rice, corn, wheat). The planting of these foods wipe out other habitats and push those animals into other habitats causing overpopulation or extinction.

Fuel sources - strip mining and the overuse of oil reserves have depleted these resources. At the current rate of consumption, conservation or alternate fuel sources will guarantee our future as a species.

Pollution - although technology gives us many advances, pollution is a side effect of production. Waste disposal and the burning of fossil fuels have polluted our land, water and air. Global warming and acid rain are two results of the burning of hydrocarbons and sulfur.

Global warming - rainforest depletion and the use of fossil fuels and aerosols have caused an increase in carbon dioxide production. This leads to a decrease in the amount of oxygen which is directly proportional to the amount of ozone. As the ozone layer depletes, more heat enters our atmosphere and is trapped. This causes an overall warming effect which may eventually melt polar ice caps, causing a rise in water levels and changes in climate which will affect weather systems.

Endangered species - construction to house our overpopulated world has caused a destruction of habitat for other animals leading to extinction.

Overpopulation - the human race is still growing at an exponential rate. Carrying capacity has not been met due to our ability to use technology to produce more food and housing. Space and water can not be manufactured and eventually our overuse affects every living thing on this planet.

SKILL 4.22 Identify the biotic and abiotic factors that influence population density.

Biotic factors - living things in an ecosystem; plants, animals, bacteria, fungi, etc. If one population in a community increases, it affects the ability of another population to succeed by limiting the available amount of food, water, shelter and space.

Abiotic factors - non-living aspects of an ecosystem; soil quality, rainfall, temperature. Changes in climate and soil can cause effects at the beginning of the food chain, thus limiting or accelerating the growth of population.

SKILL 4.23 Identify the structure and function of organs and systems of the human body.

Skeletal System - The skeletal system functions in support. Vertebrates have an endoskeleton, with muscles attached to bones. Skeletal proportions are controlled by area to volume relationships. Body size and shape is limited due to the forces of gravity. Surface area is increased to improve efficiency in all organ systems.

The **axial skeleton** consists of the bones of the skull and vertebrae. The appendicular skeleton consists of the bones of the legs, arms and tail and shoulder girdle. Bone is a connective tissue. Parts of the bone include compact bone which gives strength, spongy bone which contains red marrow to make blood cells, yellow marrow in the center of long bones to store fat cells, and the periosteum which is the protective covering on the outside of the bone.

A **joint** is defined as a place where two bones meet. Joints enable movement. Ligaments attach bone to bone. Tendons attach bones to muscles.

Muscular System - function is for movement. There are three types of muscle tissue. Skeletal muscle is voluntary. These muscles are attached to bones. Smooth muscle is involuntary. It is found in organs and enable functions such as digestion and respiration. Cardiac muscle is a specialized type of smooth muscle and is found in the heart. Muscles can only contract; therefore they work in antagonistic pairs to allow back and forward movement. Muscle fibers are made of groups of myofibrils which are made of groups of sarcomeres. Actin and myosin are proteins which make up the sarcomere.

Physiology of muscle contraction - A nerve impulse strikes a muscle fiber. This causes calcium ions to flood the sarcomere. Calcium ions allow ATP to expend energy. The myosin fibers creep along the actin, causing the muscle to contract. Once the nerve impulse has passed, calcium is pumped out and the contraction ends.

Nervous System - The neuron is the basic unit of the nervous system. It consists of an axon, which carries impulses away from the cell body, the dendrite, which carries impulses toward the cell body and the cell body, which contains the nucleus. Synapses are spaces between neurons. Chemicals called neurotransmitters are found close to the synapse. The myelin sheath, composed of Schwann cells cover the neurons and provide insulation.

Physiology of the nerve impulse - Nerve action depends on depolarization and an imbalance of electrical charges across the neuron. A polarized nerve has a positive charge outside the neuron. A depolarized nerve has a negative charge outside the neuron. Neurotransmitters turn off the sodium pump which results in depolarization of the membrane. This wave of depolarization (as it moves from neuron to neuron) carries an electrical impulse. This is actually a wave of opening and closing gates that allows for the flow of ions across the synapse. Nerves have an action potential. There is a threshold of the level of chemicals that must be met or exceeded in order for muscles to respond. This is called the "all or none" response.

The **reflex arc** is the simplest nerve response. The brain is bypassed. When a stimulus (like touching a hot stove) occurs, sensors in the hand send the message directly to the spinal cord. This stimulates motor neurons that contract the muscles to move the hand.

Voluntary nerve responses involve the brain. Receptor cells send the message to sensory neurons which lead to association neurons. The message is taken to the brain. Motor neurons are stimulated and the message is transmitted to effector cells which cause the end effect.

Organization of the Nervous System - The somatic nervous system is controlled consciously. It consists of the central nervous system (brain and spinal cord) and the peripheral nervous system (nerves that extend from the spinal cord to the muscles). The autonomic nervous system is unconsciously controlled by the hypothalamus of the brain. Smooth muscles, the heart and digestion are some processes controlled by the autonomic nervous system. It works in opposition. The sympathetic nervous system works opposite of the parasympathetic nervous system. For example, if the sympathetic nervous system stimulates an action, the parasympathetic nervous system would end that action.

Neurotransmitters - these are chemicals released by exocytosis. Some neurotransmitters stimulate, others inhibit action.

Acetylcholine - the most common neurotransmitter; it controls muscle contraction and heartbeat. The enzyme acetylcholinesterase breaks it down to end the transmission.

Epinephrine - responsible for the "fight or flight" reaction. It causes an increase in heart rate and blood flow to prepare the body for action. It is also called adrenaline.

Endorphins and enkephalins - these are natural pain killers and are released during serious injury and childbirth.

Digestive System - The function of the digestive system is to break food down and absorb it into the blood stream where it can be delivered to all cells of the body for use in cellular respiration. The teeth and saliva begin digestion by breaking food down into smaller pieces and lubricating it so it can be swallowed. The lips, cheeks and tongue form a bolus or ball of food. It is carried down the pharynx by the process of peristalsis (wave like contractions) and enters the stomach through the cardiac sphincter which closes to keep food from going back up. In the stomach, pepsinogen and hydrochloric acid form pepsin, the enzyme that breaks down proteins. The food is broken down further by this chemical action and is churned to for chyme. The pyloric sphincter muscle opens to allow the food to enter the small intestine. Most nutrient absorption occurs in the small intestine. Its large surface area, accomplished by its length and protrusions called villi and microvilli allow for a great absorptive surface into the bloodstream. Chyme is neutralized after coming from the acidic stomach to allow the enzymes found there to function. Any food left after the trip through the small intestine enters the large intestine. The large intestine functions to reabsorb water and produce vitamin K. The feces, or remaining waste, are passed out through the anus.

> **Accessory organs** - although not part of the digestive tract, these organs function in the production of necessary enzymes and bile. The pancreas makes many enzymes to break down food in the small intestine. The liver makes bile which breaks down and emulsifies fatty acids

Respiratory System - This system functions in the gas exchange of needed oxygen and carbon dioxide waste. It delivers oxygen to the bloodstream and picks up carbon dioxide for release out of the body. Air enters the mouth and nose, where it is warmed, moistened and filtered of dust and particles. Cilia in the trachea trap unwanted material in mucus, which can be expelled. The trachea splits into two bronchial tubes and the bronchial tubes divide into smaller and smaller bronchioles in the lungs. The internal surface of the lung is composed of alveoli, which are thin walled air sacs. These allow for a large surface area for gas exchange. The alveoli are lined with capillaries. Oxygen diffuses into the bloodstream and carbon dioxide diffuses out to be exhaled out of the lungs. The oxygenated blood is carried to the heart and delivered to all parts of the body.

The thoracic cavity holds the lungs. A muscle, the diaphragm, below the lungs is an adaptation that makes inhalation possible. As the volume of the thoracic cavity increases, the diaphragm muscle flattens out and inhalation occurs. When the diaphragm relaxes, exhalation occurs.

GENERAL SCIENCE

Circulatory System

The function of the circulatory system is to carry oxygenated blood and nutrients to all cells of the body and return carbon dioxide waste to be expelled from the lungs. Be familiar with the parts of the heart and the path blood takes from the heart to the lungs, through the body and back to the heart. In short, unoxygenated blood enters the heart through the inferior and superior vena cava. The first chamber it encounters is the right atrium. It goes through the tricuspid valve to the right ventricle to the pulmonary arteries and then to the lungs where it is oxygenated. It returns to the heart through the pulmonary vein into the left atrium. It travels through the bicuspid valve to the left ventricle where it is pumped to all parts of the body through the aorta.

Sinoatrial node (SA node) - the pacemaker of the heart. Located on the right atrium, it is responsible for contraction of the right and left atrium.

Atrioventricular node (AV node) - located on the left ventricle, it is responsible for contraction of the ventricles.

Blood vessels include:

arteries - lead away from the heart. All arteries carry oxygenated blood except the pulmonary artery going to the lungs. Arteries are under high pressure.

arterioles - arteries branch off to form smaller arterioles.

capillaries - arterioles branch off to form tiny capillaries that reach every cell. Blood moves slowest here due to the small size; only one red blood cell may pass at a time to allow for diffusion of gases into and out of cells. Nutrients are also absorbed by the cells from the capillaries.

venules - capillaries combine to form larger venules. The vessels are now carrying waste products from the cells.

veins - venules combine to form larger veins, leading back to the heart. Veins and venules have thinner walls than arteries because t They are not under as much pressure. Veins contain valves to prevent the backward flow of blood due to gravity.

Components of the blood include:

plasma – 60% of the blood is plasma. It contains salts called electrolytes, nutrients and waste. It is the liquid part of blood.

erythrocytes - also called red blood cells; they contain hemoglobin which carries oxygen molecules.

leukocytes - also called white blood cells. White blood cells are larger than red cells. They are phagocytic and can engulf invaders. White blood cells are not confined to the blood vessels and can enter the interstitial fluid between cells.

platelets - assist in blood clotting. Platelets are made in the bone marrow.

Blood clotting - the neurotransmitter that initiates blood vessel constriction following an injury is called serotonin. A material called prothrombin is converted to thrombin with the help of thromboplastin. The thrombin is then used to convert fibrinogen to fibrin which traps red blood cells to form a scab and stop blood flow.

Lymphatic System (Immune System)

Nonspecific defense mechanisms – They do not target specific pathogens, but are a whole body response. Results of nonspecific mechanisms are seen as symptoms of an infection. These mechanisms include the skin, mucous membranes and cells of the blood and lymph (ie: white blood cells, macrophages). Fever is a result of an increase of white blood cells. Pyrogens are released by white blood cells which set the body's thermostat to a higher temperature. This inhibits the growth of microorganisms. It also increases metabolism to increase phagocytosis and body repair.

Specific defense mechanisms - They recognize foreign material and responds by destroying the invader. These mechanisms are specific and diverse. They are able to recognize individual pathogens. They also have recognition of foreign material versus the self. Memory of the invaders provides immunity upon further exposure.

antigen - any foreign particle that invades the body.
antibody - manufactured by the body, they recognize and latch onto antigens, hopefully destroying them.
immunity - this is the body's ability to recognize and destroy an antigen before it causes harm. Active immunity develops after recovery from an infectious disease (chicken pox) or after a vaccination (mumps, measles, rubella). Passive immunity may be passed from one individual to another. It is not permanent. A good example is the immunities passed from mother to nursing child.

Excretory System

The function of the excretory system is to rid the body of nitrogenous wastes in the form of urea. The functional unit of excretion is the nephron, which make up the kidneys. Antidiuretic hormone (ADH) which is made in the hypothalamus and stored in the pituitary is released when differences in osmotic balance occur. This will cause more water to be reabsorbed. As the blood becomes more dilute, ADH release ends.

The Bowman,s capsule contains the glomerulus, a tightly packed group of capillaries. The glomerulus is under high pressure. Waste and fluids leak out due to pressure. Filtration is not selective in this area. Selective secretion by active and passive transport occur in the proximal convoluted tubule. Unwanted molecules are secreted into the filtrate. Selective secretion also occurs in the loop of Henle. Salt is actively pumped out of the tube and much water is lost due to the hyperosmosity of the inner part (medulla) of the kidney. As the fluid enters the distal convoluted tubule, more water is reabsorbed. Urine forms in the collecting duct which leads to the ureter then to the bladder where it is stored. Urine is passed from the bladder through the urethra. The amount of water reabsorbed back into the body is dependent upon how much water or fluids an individual has consumed. Urine can be very dilute or very concentrated if dehydration is present.

Endocrine System

The function of the endocrine system is to manufacture proteins called hormones. Hormones are released into the bloodstream and are carried to a target tissue where they stimulate an action. Hormones may build up over time to cause their effect, as in puberty or the menstrual cycle.

Hormone activation - Hormones are specific and fit receptors on the target tissue cell surface. The receptor activates an enzyme which converts ATP to cyclic AMP. Cyclic AMP (cAMP) is a second messenger from the cell membrane to the nucleus. The genes found in the nucleus turn on or off to cause a specific response.

There are two classes of hormones. **Steroid hormones** come from cholesterol. Steroid hormones cause sexual characteristics and mating behavior. Hormones include estrogen and progesterone in females and testosterone in males. **Peptide hormones** are made in the pituitary, adrenal glands on the kidneys and the pancreas. They include the following:

Follicle stimulating hormone (FSH) - production of sperm or egg cells

Luteinizing hormone (LH) - functions in ovulation

Luteotropic hormone (LTH) - assists in production of progesterone

Growth hormone (GH) - stimulates growth

Antidiuretic hormone (ADH) - assists in retention of water

Oxytocin - stimulates labor contractions at birth and let-down of milk

Melatonin - regulates circadian rhythms and seasonal changes

Epinephrine (adrenalin) - causes fight or flight reaction of the nervous system

Thyroxin - increases metabolic rate

Calcitonin - removes calcium from the blood

Insulin - decreases glucose level in blood

Glucagon - increases glucose level in blood

Although you probably won't be tested on individual hormones, be aware that hormones work on a feedback system. The increase or decrease in one hormone may cause the increase or decrease in another. Releasing hormones cause the release of specific hormones.

Reproductive System

Sexual reproduction greatly increases diversity due to the many combinations possible through meiosis and fertilization. Gametogenesis is the production of the sperm and egg cells. Spermatogenesis begins at puberty in the male. One spermatozoa produces four sperm. The sperm mature in the seminiferous tubules located in the testes. Oogenesis, the production of egg cells is usually complete by the birth of a female. Egg cells are not released until menstruation begins at puberty. Meiosis forms one ovum with all the cytoplasm and three polar bodies which are reabsorbed by the body. The ovum are stored in the ovaries and released each month from puberty to menopause.

Path of the sperm - sperm are stored in the seminiferous tubules in the testes where they mature. Mature sperm are found in the epididymis located on top of the testes. After ejaculation, the sperm travels up the vas deferens where they mix with semen made in the prostate and seminal vesicles and travel out the urethra.

Path of the egg - eggs are stored in the ovaries. Ovulation releases the egg into the fallopian tubes which are ciliated to move the egg along. Fertilization normally occurs in the fallopian tube. If pregnancy does not occur, the egg passes through the uterus and is expelled through the vagina during menstruation. Levels of progesterone and estrogen stimulate menstruation and are affected by the implantation of a fertilized egg so menstruation does not occur.

Pregnancy - if fertilization occurs, the zygote implants in about two to three days in the uterus. Implantation promotes secretion of human chorionic gonadotrophin (HCG). This is what is detected in pregnancy tests. The HCG keeps the level of progesterone elevated to maintain the uterine lining in order to feed the developing embryo until the umbilical cord forms. Labor is initiated by oxytocin which causes labor contractions and dilation of the cervix. Prolactin and oxytocin cause the production of milk.

SKILL 4.24   Identify the substances that are helpful or harmful in the care and maintenance of the body.

Good nutrition is paramount in maintaining health for growth and development. A balanced diet includes foods from the major food groups of carbohydrates, proteins, lipids and sufficient quantities of vitamins and minerals.

Body pollutants, such as tobacco, drugs and alcohol interfere with the absorption of nutrients and also may interfere with physical and mental development. They may also damage developing organs, leading to lifelong diseases such as emphysema or asthma.

COMPETENCY 5.0 KNOWLEDGE OF PHYSICS

SKILL 5.1 **Distinguish between temperature and heat and their measurements.**

Heat and temperature are different physical quantities. **Heat** is a measure of energy. **Temperature** is the measure of how hot (or cold) a body is with respect to a standard object.

Two concepts are important in the discussion of temperature changes. Objects are in thermal contact if they can affect each other's temperatures. Set a hot cup of coffee on a desk top. The two objects are in thermal contact with each other and will begin affecting each other's temperatures. The coffee will become cooler and the desktop warmer. Eventually, they will have the same temperature. When this happens, they are in **thermal equilibrium.**

We can not rely on our sense of touch to determine temperature because the heat from a hand may be conducted more efficiently by certain objects, making them feel colder. **Thermometers** are used to measure temperature. A small amount of mercury in a capillary tube will expand when heated. The thermometer and the object whose temperature it is measuring are put in contact long enough for them to reach thermal equilibrium. Then the temperature can be read from the thermometer scale.

Three temperature scales are used:

Celsius: The freezing point of water is set at 0 and the steam (boiling) point is 100. The interval between the two is divided into 100 equal parts called degrees Celsius.

Fahrenheit: The freezing point of water is 32 degrees and the boiling point is 212. The interval between is divided into 180 equal parts called degrees Fahrenheit.

Temperature readings can be converted from one to the other as follows.

Fahrenheit to Celsius	**Celsius to Fahrenheit**
$C = 5/9\,(F - 32)$	$F = (9/5)\,C + 32$

Kelvin Scale has the degrees the same size as the Celsius scale, but the zero point is moved to the triple point of water. Water inside a closed vessel is in thermal equilibrium in all three states (ice, water, and vapor) at 273.15 degrees Kelvin. This temperature is equivalent to .01 degrees Celsius. Because the degrees are the same in the two scales, temperature changes are the same in Celsius and Kelvin.

Temperature readings can be converted from Celsius to Kelvin:

Celsius to Kelvin	**Kelvin to Celsius**
$K = C + 273.15$	$C = K - 273.15$

Heat is a measure of energy. If two objects that have different temperatures come into contact with each other, heat flows from the hotter object to the cooler.

Heat Capacity of an object is the amount of heat energy that it takes to raise the temperature of the object by one degree.

Heat capacity (C) per unit mass (m) is called **specific heat** (c):

$$c = \frac{C}{m} = \frac{Q/\Delta}{m}$$

Specific heats for many materials have been calculated and can be found in tables.

There are a number of ways that heat is measured. In each case, the measurement is dependent upon raising the temperature of a specific amount of water by a specific amount. These conversions of heat energy and work are called the **mechanical equivalent of heat**.

The **calorie** is the amount of energy that it takes to raise one gram of water one degree.

The **kilocalorie** is the amount of energy that it takes to raise one kilogram of water by one degree Celsius. Food calories are kilocalories.

In the International System of Units **(SI)**, the calorie is equal to 4.184 **joules**.

British thermal units (BTU) - (BTU = 252 calories = 1.054 kJ)

SKILL 5.2   Identify the types of heat transfer and their characteristics.

Heat energy that is transferred into or out of a system is **heat transfer.** The temperature change is positive for a gain in heat energy and negative when heat is removed from the object or system.

The formula for heat transfer is $Q = mc\Delta T$ where Q is the amount of heat energy transferred, m is the amount of substance (in kilograms), c is the specific heat of the substance, and ΔT is the change in temperature of the substance. It is important to assume that the objects in thermal contact are isolated and insulated from their surroundings.

If a substance in a closed container loses heat, then another substance in the container must gain heat.

A **calorimeter** uses the transfer of heat from one substance to another to determine the specific heat of the substance.

When an object undergoes a change of phase it goes from one physical state (solid, liquid, or gas) to another. For instance, water can go from liquid to solid (freezing) or from liquid to gas (boiling). The heat that is required to change from one state to the other is called **latent heat.**

The **heat of fusion** is the amount of heat that it takes to change from a solid to a liquid or the amount of heat released during the change from liquid to solid.

The **heat of vaporization** is the amount of heat that it takes to change from a liquid to a gaseous state.

Heat is transferred in three ways: **conduction, convection, and radiation.**

Conduction occurs when heat travels through the heated solid.

The transfer rate is the ratio of the amount of heat per amount of time it takes to transfer heat from area of an object to another. For example, if you place an iron pan on a flame, the handle will eventually become hot. How fast the handle gets too hot to handle is a function of the amount of heat and how long it is applied. Because the change in time is in the denominator of the function, the shorter the amount of time it takes to heat the handle, the greater the transfer rate.

Convection is heat transported by the movement of a heated substance. Warmed air rising from a heat source such as a fire or electric heater is a common example of convection. Convection ovens make use of circulating air to more efficiently cook food.

Radiation is heat transfer as the result of electromagnetic waves. The sun warms the earth by emitting radiant energy.

An example of all three methods of heat transfer occurs in the thermos bottle or Dewar flask. The bottle is constructed of double walls of Pyrex glass that have a space in between. Air is evacuated from the space between the walls and the inner wall is silvered. The lack of air between the walls lessens heat loss by convection and conduction. The heat inside is reflected by the silver, cutting down heat transfer by radiation. Hot liquids remain hotter and cold liquids remain colder longer.

SKILL 5.3   Identify the laws of thermodynamics and the related concepts of molecular motion and thermal expansion.

The relationship between heat and forms of energy and work (mechanical, electrical, etc.) are the **Laws of Thermodynamics.** These laws deal strictly with systems in thermal equilibrium and not those with in the process of rapid change or in a state of transition. Systems that are nearly always in a state of equilibrium are called **reversible systems.**

The first law of thermodynamics is a restatement of conservation of energy. The change in heat energy supplied to a system (Q) is equal to the sum of the change in the internal energy (U) and the change in the work done by the system against internal forces (W). $\Delta Q = \Delta U + \Delta W$

The second law of thermodynamics is stated in two parts:

1. No machine is 100% efficient. It is impossible to construct a machine that only absorbs heat from a heat source and performs an equal amount of work because some heat will always be lost to the environment.

2. Heat can not spontaneously pass from a colder to a hotter object. An ice cube sitting on a hot sidewalk will melt into a little puddle, but it will never spontaneously cool and form the same ice cube. Certain events have a preferred direction called the **arrow of time.**

Entropy is the measure of how much energy or heat is available for work. Work occurs only when heat is transferred from hot to cooler objects. Once this is done, no more work can be extracted from them alone. The energy is still being conserved, but is not available for work as long as the objects are the same temperature. Theory has it that eventually, all things in the universe will reach the same temperature. If this happens, energy will no longer be usable.

SKILL 5.4 Identify the types and characteristics of forces, examples of Newton's laws of motion and the methods of measuring them.

Dynamics is the study of the relationship between motion and the forces affecting motion. **Force** causes motion.

Mass and weight are not the same quantities. An object's **mass** gives it a reluctance to change its current state of motion. It is also the measure of an object's resistance to acceleration. The force that the earth's gravity exerts on an object with a specific mass is called the objects weight on earth. Weight is a force that is measured in Newtons. Weight (W) = mass times acceleration due to gravity. (**W = mg**). To illustrate the difference between mass and weight, picture two rocks of equal mass on a balance scale. If the scale is balanced in one place, it will be balanced everywhere, regardless of the gravitational field. However, the weight of the stones would vary on a spring scale, depending upon the gravitational field. In other words, the stones would be balanced both on earth and on the moon. However, the weight of the stones would be greater on earth than on the moon.

Newton's laws of motion:

Newton's first law of motion is also called the law of inertia. It states that an object at rest will remain at rest and an object in motion will remain in motion at a constant velocity unless acted upon by an external force.

Newton's second law of motion states that if a net force acts on an object, it will cause the acceleration of the object. The relationship between force and motion is Force equals mass times acceleration. (**F = ma**).

Newton's third law states that for every action there is an equal and opposite reaction. Therefore, if an object exerts a force on another object, that second object exerts an equal and opposite force on the first.

Surfaces that touch each other have a certain resistance to motion. This resistance is **friction.**

1. The materials that make up the surfaces will determine the magnitude of the frictional force.
2. The frictional force is independent of the area of contact between the two surfaces.
3. The direction of the frictional force is opposite to the direction of motion.
4. The frictional force is proportional to the normal force between the two surfaces in contact.

GENERAL SCIENCE

Static friction describes the force of friction of two surfaces that are in contact but do not have any motion relative to each other, such as a block sitting on an inclined plane. **Kinetic friction** describes the force of friction of two surfaces in contact with each other when there is relative motion between the surfaces

When an object moves in a circular path, a force must be directed toward the center of the circle in order to keep the motion going. This constraining force is called **centripetal force**. Gravity is the centripetal force that keeps a satellite circling the earth.

SKILL 5.5   Apply knowledge of forces and motion to solve problems.

Use section 5.5 along with any physics classes or kinesiology classes to solve problems regarding buoyancy, centripetal force, elastic force, electric force, force on moving objects, muscular force, force on objects at rest, gravitational, simple machines and force, and work and force.

Push and pulls –Pushing a volleyball or pulling a bowstring applies muscular force when the muscles expand and contract. When the bow is released it is elastic force when any object returns to its original shape.

Rubbing – Friction opposes the motion of one surface past another. Friction is common when slowing down a car.

Pull of gravity – is a force of attraction between two objects. Gravity questions can be raised not only on earth but also between planets and even black hole discussions.

Forces on objects at rest – The formula $F = m/a$ means that a force equals mass over acceleration. An object will not move unless the force is strong enough to move the mass. Also there can be opposing forces holding the object in place. For instance a boat may want to be forced by the currents to drift away but an equal and opposite force is a rope holding it to a dock.

Forces on a moving object - Overcoming inertia is the tendency of any object to oppose a change in motion. An object at rest tends to stay at rest. An object that is moving tends to keep moving.

Inertia and circular motion – The centripetal force is provided by the high banking of the curved road and by friction between the wheels and the road. This inward force keeps an object moving in a circle is centripetal force.

SKILL 5.6   Identify simple machines.

1. Inclined plane
2. Lever
3. Wheel and axle
4. Pulley

SKILL 5.7   Apply knowledge of simple machines to solve problems involving work, power, mechanical advantage, and efficiency.

Work and energy:

Work is done on an object when an applied force moves through a distance.

Power is the work done divided by the amount of time that it took to do it. (Power = Work / time)

SKILL 5.8   Identify the process by which sound is produced and transmitted.

Sound waves are produced by a vibrating body. The vibrating object moves forward and compresses the air in front of it, then reverses direction so that the pressure on the air is lessened and expansion of the air molecules occurs. One compression and expansion creates one longitudinal wave. Sound can be transmitted through any gas, liquid, or solid. However, it cannot be transmitted through a vacuum, because there are no particles present to vibrate and bump into their adjacent particles to transmit the waves.

The vibrating air molecules move back and forth parallel to the direction of motion of the wave as they pass the energy from adjacent air molecules closer to the source to air molecules farther away from the source.

SKILL 5.9   Identify the characteristics of the components of a sound wave and methods for their measurements.

The **pitch** of a sound depends on the **frequency** that the ear receives. High-pitched sound waves have high frequencies. High notes are produced by an object that is vibrating at a greater number of times per second than one that produces a low note.

The **intensity** of a sound is the amount of energy that crosses a unit of area in a given unit of time. The loudness of the sound is subjective and depends upon the effect on the human ear. Two tones of the same intensity but different pitches may appear to have different loudness. The intensity level of sound is measured in decibels. Normal conversation is about 60 decibels. A power saw is about 110 decibels.

The **amplitude** of a sound wave determines its loudness. Loud sound waves have large amplitudes. The larger the sound wave, the more energy is needed to create the wave.

An oscilloscope is useful in studying waves because it gives a picture of the wave that shows the crest and trough of the waves. **Interference** is the interaction of two or more waves that meet. If the waves interfere constructively, the crest of each one meets the crests of the others. They combine into a crest with greater amplitude. As a result, you hear a louder sound. If the waves interfere destructively, then the crest of one meets the trough of another. They produce a wave with lower amplitude that produces a softer sound.

If you have two tuning forks that produce different pitches, then one will produce sounds of a slightly higher frequency. When you strike the two forks simultaneously, you may hear beats. **Beats** are a series of loud and soft sounds. This is because when the waves meet, the crests combine at some points and produce loud sounds. At other points, they nearly cancel each other out and produce soft sounds.

SKILL 5.10 Apply the characteristics of sound as they apply to everyday situations (e.g. music, noise, and the Doppler Effect).

When a piano tuner tunes a piano, he only uses one tuning fork, even though there are many strings on the piano. He adjusts to first string to be the same as that of the tuning fork. Then he listens to the beats that occur when both the tuned and untuned strings are struck. He adjusts the untuned string until he can hear the correct number of beats per second. This process of striking the untuned and tuned strings together and timing the beats is repeated until all the piano strings are tuned.

Pleasant sounds have a regular wave pattern that is repeated over and over. Sounds that have an irregular that do not happen with regularity are unpleasant and are called **noise**.

Change in experienced frequency due to relative motion of the source of the sound is called the **Doppler Effect.** When a siren approaches, the pitch is high. When it passes, the pitch drops. As a moving sound source approaches a listener, the sound waves are closer together, causing an increase in frequency in the sound that is heard. As the source passes the listener, the waves spread out and the frequency experienced by the listener is lower.

SKILL 5.11 Identify the principles relating to the changing pathways of light.

Shadows illustrate on of the basic properties of light. Light travels in a straight line. If you put your hand between a light source and a wall, you will interrupt the light and produce a shadow.

When light hits a surface, it is **reflected.** The angle of the incoming light - the angle of incidence - is the same as the angle of the reflected light - the angle of reflection. It is this reflected light that allows you to see objects. You see the objects when the reflected light reaches your eyes.

Different surfaces reflect light differently. Rough surfaces scatter light in many different directions. A smooth surface reflects the light in one direction. If it is smooth and shiny (like a mirror) reflection allows you to see your image in the surface.

When light enters a different medium, it bends. This bending, or change of speed, is called **refraction**.

Light can be **diffracted**, or bent around the edges of an object. Diffraction occurs when light goes through a narrow slit. As light passes through it, the light bends slightly around the edges of the slit. You can demonstrate this by pressing your thumb and forefinger together, making a very thin slit between them. Hold them about 8 cm from your eye and look at a distant source of light. The pattern you observe is caused by the diffraction of light.

SKILL 5.12 Apply knowledge of light and optics to practical applications, such as eyeglasses, other optical instruments, and communication.

Light and other electromagnetic radiation can be polarized because the waves are transverse. The distinguishing characteristic of transverse waves is that they are perpendicular to the direction of the motion of the wave. Polarized light has vibrations confined to a single plane that is perpendicular to the direction of motion. Light is able to be polarized by passing it through special filters that block all vibrations except those in a single plane. By blocking out all but one place of vibration, polarized sunglasses cut down on glare.

Light can travel through thin fibers of glass or plastic without escaping the sides. Light on the inside of these fibers is reflected so that it stays inside the fiber until it reaches the other end. Such fiber optics are being used to carry telephone messages. Sound waves are converted to electric signals which are coded into a series of light pulses which move through the optical fiber until they reach the other end. At that time, they are converted back into sound.

The image that you see in a bathroom mirror is a virtual image because it only seems to be where it is. However, a curved mirror can produce a real image. A real image is produce when light passes through the point where the image appears. A real image can be projected onto a screen.

Cameras use a convex lens to produce an image on the film. A **convex lens** is thicker in the middle than at the edges. The image size depends upon the focal length (distance from the focus to the lens). The longer the focal length, the larger the image. A **converging lens** produces a real image whenever the object is far enough from the lens so that the rays of light from the object can hit the lens and be focused into a real image on the other side of the lens.

Eyeglasses can help correct sight defects by changing where the image seen is focused on the retina of the eye. If a person is nearsighted, the lens of his eye focuses images in front of the retina. In this case, the corrective lens placed in the eyeglasses will be concave so that the image will reach the retina. In the case of farsightedness, the lens of the eye focuses the image behind the retina. The correction will call for a convex lens to be fitted into the glass frames so that the image is brought forward into sharper focus.

SKILL 5.13 Identify the parts of the electromagnetic spectrum and the relative wavelengths and energy associated with each.

The electromagnetic spectrum is measured in frequency (f) in hertz and wavelength (λ) in meters. The frequency times the wavelength of every electromagnetic wave equals the speed of light (3.0×10^9 meters/second).

Roughly, the range of wavelengths of the electromagnetic spectrum is:

	f	λ
Radio waves	$10^{5} - 10^{-1}$ meters	$10^{3} - 10^{9}$ hertz
Microwaves	$10^{-1} - 10^{-3}$ meters	$10^{9} - 10^{11}$ hertz
Infrared radiation	$10^{-3} - 10^{-6}$ meters	$10^{11.2} - 10^{14.3}$ hertz
Visible light	$10^{-6.2} - 10^{-6.9}$ meters	$10^{14.3} - 10^{15}$ hertz
Ultraviolet radiation	$10^{-7} - 10^{-9}$ meters	$10^{15} - 10^{17.2}$ hertz
X-Rays	$10^{-9} - 10^{-11}$ meters	$10^{17.2} - 10^{19}$ hertz
Gamma Rays	$10^{-11} - 10^{-15}$ meters	$10^{19} - 10^{23.25}$ hertz

　GENERAL SCIENCE

SKILL 5.14 Identify characteristics and examples of static electricity and charged objects.

Electrostatics is the study of stationary electric charges. A plastic rod that is rubbed with fur or a glass rod that is rubbed with silk will become electrically charged and will attract small pieces of paper. The charge on the plastic rod rubbed with fur is negative and the charge on glass rod rubbed with silk is positive.

Electrically charged objects share these characteristics:

1. Like charges repel one another.
2. Opposite charges attract each other.
3. Charge is conserved. A neutral object has no net change. If the plastic rod and fur are initially neutral, when the rod becomes charged by the fur a negative charge is transferred from the fur to the rod. The net negative charge on the rod is equal to the net positive charge on the fur.

Materials through which electric charges can easily flow are called conductors. On the other hand, an **insulator** is a material through which electric charges do not move easily, if at all. A simple device used to indicate the existence of a positive or negative charge is called an **electroscope**. An electroscope is made up of a conducting knob and attached very lightweight conducting leaves - usually made of gold foil or aluminum foil. When a charged object touches the knob, the leaves push away from each other because like charges repel. It is not possible to tell whether or not the charge is positive or negative.

Charging by induction:

Touch the knob with a finger while a charged rod is nearby. The electrons will be repulsed and flow out of the electroscope through the hand. If the hand is removed while the charged rod remains close, the electroscope will retain the charge.

When an object is rubbed with a charged rod, the object will take on the same charge as the rod. However, charging by induction gives the object the opposite charge as that of the charged rod.

Grounding charge:

Charge can be removed from an object by connecting it to the earth through a conductor. The removal of static electricity by conduction is called **grounding**.

SKILL 5.15 Identify types, characteristics, and methods of measuring current and circuits.

An **electric circuit** is a path along which electrons flow. A simple circuit can be created with a dry cell, wire, and a bell, or light bulb. When all are connected, the electrons flow from the negative terminal, through the wire to the device and back to the positive terminal of the dry cell. If there are no breaks in the circuit, the device will work. The circuit is closed. Any break in the flow will create an open circuit and cause the device to shut off.

The device (bell, bulb) is an example of a **load**. A load is a device that uses energy. Suppose that you also add a buzzer so that the bell rings when you press the buzzer button. The buzzer is acting as a **switch**. A switch is a device that opens or closes a circuit. Pressing the buzzer makes the connection complete and the bell rings. When the buzzer is not engaged, the circuit is open and the bell is silent.

A **series circuit** is one where the electrons have only one path along which they can move. When one load in a series circuit goes out, the circuit is open. An example of this is a set of Christmas tree lights that is missing a bulb. None of the bulbs will work.

A **parallel circuit** is one where the electrons have more than one path to move along. Each path is known as a path. If a load goes out in a parallel circuit, the other load will still work because the electrons can still find a way to continue moving along the path.

When an electron goes through a load, it does work and therefore loses some of its energy. The measure of how much energy is lost is called the **potential difference**. The potential difference between two points is the work needed to move a charge from one point to another.

Potential difference is measured in a unit called the volt. **Voltage** is potential difference. The higher the voltage, the more energy the electrons have. This energy is measured by a device called a voltmeter. To use a voltmeter, place it in a circuit parallel with the load you are measuring.

Current is the number of electrons per second that flow past a point in a circuit. Current is measured with a device called an ammeter. To use an ammeter, put it in series with the load you are measuring.

As electrons flow through a wire, they lose potential energy. Some is changed into heat energy because of resistance. **Resistance** is the ability of the material to oppose the flow of electrons through it. All substances have some resistance, even if they are a good conductor such as copper. This resistance is measured in units called **ohms**. A thin wire will have more resistance than a thick one because it will have less room for electrons to travel. In a thicker wire, there will be more possible paths for the electrons to flow. Resistance also depends upon the length of the wire. The longer the wire, the more resistance it will have. Potential difference, resistance, and current form a relationship know as **Ohm's Law**. Current **(I)** is equal to potential difference **(V)** divided by resistance **(R)**.

$$I = V / R$$

If you have a wire with resistance of 5 ohms and a potential difference of 75 volts, you can calculate the current by

I = 75 volts / 5 ohms
I = 15 amperes

A current of 10 or more amperes will cause a wire to get hot. 22 amperes is about the maximum for a house circuit. Anything above 25 amperes can start a fire.

SKILL 5.16 Apply knowledge of currents, circuits, conductors, insulators, and resistors to everyday situations.

Electricity can be used to change the chemical composition of a material. For instance, when electricity is passed through water, it breaks the water down into hydrogen gas and oxygen gas.

Circuit breakers in a home monitor the electric current. If there is an overload, the circuit breaker will create an open circuit, stopping the flow of electricity.

Computers can be made small enough to fit inside a plastic credit card by creating what is known as a solid state device. In this device, electrons flow through solid material such as silicon.

Resistors are used to regulate volume on a television or radio or through a dimmer switch for lights.

A bird can sit on an electrical wire without being electrocuted because the bird and the wire have about the same potential. However, if that same bird would touch two wires at the same time he would not have to worry about flying south next year.

When caught in an electrical storm, a car is a relatively safe place from lightening because of the resistance of the rubber tires. A metal building would not be safe unless there was a lightening rod that would attract the lightening and conduct it to the ground.

SKILL 5.17   Identify characteristics of types of magnets, magnetic fields, and compasses.

Magnets have a north pole and a south pole. Like poles repel and different poles attract. A **magnetic field** is the space around a magnet where its force will affect objects. The closer you are to a magnet, the stronger the force. As you move away, the force becomes weaker.

Some materials act as magnets and some do not. This is because magnetism is a result of electrons in motion. The most important motion in this case is the spinning of the individual electrons. Electrons spin in pairs in opposite directions in most atoms. Each spinning electron has the magnetic field that it creates canceled out by the electron that is spinning in the opposite direction.

In an atom of iron, there are four unpaired electrons. The magnetic fields of these are not canceled out. Their fields add up to make a tiny magnet. There fields exert forces on each other setting up small areas in the iron called **magnetic domains** where atomic magnetic fields line up in the same direction.

You can make a magnet out of an iron nail by stroking the nail in the same direction repeatedly with a magnet. This causes poles in the atomic magnets in the nail to be attracted to the magnet. The tiny magnetic fields in the nail line up in the direction of the magnet. The magnet causes the domains pointing in its direction in the nail to grow. Eventually, one large domain results and the nail becomes a magnet.

A bar magnet has a north pole and a south pole. If you break the magnet in half, each piece will have a north and south pole.

The earth has a magnetic field. In a compass, a tiny, lightweight magnet is suspended and will line its south pole up with the North Pole magnet of the earth.

A magnet can be made out of a coil of wire by connecting the ends of the coil to a battery. When the current goes through the wire, the wire acts in the same way that a magnet does, it is called an **electromagnet**.

The poles of the electromagnet will depend upon which way the electric current runs. An electromagnet can be made more powerful in three ways:

1. Make more coils.
2. Put an iron core (nail) inside the coils.
3. Use more battery power.

SKILL 5.18 Apply knowledge of magnets and magnetic fields to everyday situations.

Telegraphs use electromagnets to work. When a telegraph key is pushed, current flows through a circuit, turning on an electromagnet which attracts an iron bar. The iron bar hits a sounding board which responds with a click. Release the key and the electromagnet turns off. Messages can be sent around the world in this way.

Scrap metal can be removed from waste materials by the use of a large electromagnet that is suspended from a crane. When the electromagnet is turned on, the metal in the pile of waste will be attracted to it. All other materials will stay on the ground.

Air conditioners, vacuum cleaners, and washing machines use electric motors. An electric motor uses an electromagnet to change electric energy into mechanical energy.

SKILL 5.19 Distinguish between fission and fusion and the resulting radioactivity.

Chemical reactions involve the breaking and forming of bonds between atoms. Bonds involve only the outer electrons and do not affect the nucleus. When a reaction involves a nucleus, elements are changed into different elements. This is called a **nuclear reaction**.

The binding energy is released when the nuclei of atoms are split apart in a nuclear reaction. This binding energy is called **nuclear energy**.

There are two types of nuclear reactions:

Nuclear fission occurs when the nuclei are split apart. Smaller nuclei are formed and energy is released. The fission of many atoms in a short time period releases a large amount of energy. "Heavy water" is used in a nuclear reactor to slow down neutrons, controlling and moderating the nuclear reactions. Controlling the release so that energy is released slowly gives us nuclear submarines and nuclear power plants.

Nuclear fusion is the opposite. It occurs when small nuclei combine to form a larger nucleus. It begins with the hydrogen atom, which has the smallest nuclei. During one type of fusion, four hydrogen nuclei are fused at very high pressures and temperatures. They form one helium atom. The sun and stars are examples of fusion. They are made mostly of hydrogen that is constantly fusing. As the hydrogen forms helium, it releases an energy that we see as light. When all of the hydrogen is used, the star will no longer shine. Scientists estimate that the sun has enough hydrogen to keep it glowing for another four billion years.

During a nuclear reaction, elements change into other elements called **radioactive elements**. Uranium is a radioactive element. The element uranium breaks down and changes into the element lead. Most natural radioactive elements breakdown slowly, so energy is released over a long period of time.

Radioactive particles are used in the treatment of cancer because they can kill cancer cells. However, if they are powerful enough, they can also cause death. People working around such substances must protect themselves with the correct clothing, equipment, and procedures.

This Page Intentionally Left Blank

DIRECTIONS: Read each item and select the correct response. The answer key follows.

1. In an experiment, the scientist states that he believes a change in the color of a liquid is due to a change of pH. This is an example of

   A. observing.

   B. inferring.

   C. measuring.

   D. classifying.

2. When is a hypothesis formed?

   A. Before the data is taken.

   B. After the data is taken.

   C. After the data is analyzed.

   D. Concurrent with graphing the data.

3. Who determines the laws regarding the use of safety glasses in the classroom?

   A. The state.

   B. The school site.

   C. The Federal government.

   D. The district level.

4. If one inch equals 2.54 cm how many mm in 1.5 feet? (APPROXIMATELY)

   A. 18 mm.

   B. 1800 mm.

   C. 460 mm.

   D. 4,600 mm.

5. Which of the following instruments measures wind speed?

   A. A barometer.

   B. An anemometer.

   C. A wind sock.

   D. A weather vane.

6. Sonar works by

   A. timing how long it takes sound to reach a certain speed.

   B. bouncing sound waves between two metal plates.

   C. bouncing sound waves off an underwater object and timing how long it takes for the sound to return.

   D. evaluating the motion and amplitude of sound.

7. The measure of the pull of the earth's gravity on an object is called

    A. mass number.

    B. atomic number.

    C. mass.

    D. weight.

8. Which reaction below is a decomposition reaction?

    A. $HCl + NaOH \rightarrow NaCl + H_2O$

    B. $C + O_2 \rightarrow CO_2$

    C. $2H_2O \rightarrow 2H_2 + O_2$

    D. $CuSO_4 + Fe \rightarrow FeSO_4 + Cu$

9. The Law of Conservation of Energy states that

    A. There must be the same number of products and reactants in any chemical equation.

    B. Objects always fall toward large masses such as planets.

    C. Energy is neither created nor destroyed, but may change form.

    D. Lights must be turned off when not in use, by state regulation.

10. Which parts of an atom are located inside the nucleus?

    A. electrons and neutrons.

    B. protons and neutrons.

    C. protons only.

    D. neutrons only.

11. The elements in the modern Periodic Table are arranged

    A. in numerical order by atomic number.

    B. randomly.

    C. in alphabetical order by chemical symbol.

    D. in numerical order by atomic mass.

12. Carbon bonds with hydrogen by

    A. ionic bonding.

    B. non-polar covalent bonding.

    C. polar covalent bonding.

    D. strong nuclear force.

13. Vinegar is an example of a

    A. strong acid.

    B. strong base.

    C. weak acid.

    D. weak base.

GENERAL SCIENCE

14. Which of the following is not a nucleotide?

    A. adenine.

    B. alanine.

    C. cytosine.

    D. guanine.

15. When measuring the volume of water in a graduated cylinder, where does one read the measurement?

    A. At the highest point of the liquid.

    B. At the bottom of the meniscus curve.

    C. At the closest mark to the top of the liquid.

    D. At the top of the plastic safety ring.

16. A duck's webbed feet are examples of

    A. mimicry.

    B. structural adaptation.

    C. protective resemblance.

    D. protective coloration

17. What cell organelle contains the cell's stored food?

    A. Vacuoles.

    B. Golgi Apparatus.

    C. Ribosomes.

    D. Lysosomes.

18. The first stage of mitosis is called

    A. telophase.

    B. anaphase.

    C. prophase.

    D. mitophase.

19. The Doppler Effect is associated most closely with which property of waves?

    A. amplitude.

    B. wavelength.

    C. frequency.

    D. intensity.

20. Viruses are responsible for many human diseases including all of the following *except*

    A. influenza.

    B. A.I.D.S.

    C. the common cold.

    D. strep throat.

21. A series of experiments on pea plants formed by _____ showed that two invisible markers existed for each trait and one marker dominated the other.

    A. Pasteur.

    B. Watson and Crick.

    C. Mendel.

    D. Mendeleev.

22. Formaldehyde should not be used in school laboratories for the following reason:

    A. it smells unpleasant.

    B. it is a known carcinogen.

    C. it is expensive to obtain.

    D. it is an explosive.

23. Amino acids are carried to the ribosome in protein synthesis by:

    A. transfer RNA (tRNA).

    B. messenger RNA (mRNA).

    C. ribosomal RNA (rRNA).

    D. transformation RNA (trRNA).

24. When designing a scientific experiment, a student considers all the factors that may influence the results. The process goal is to

    A. recognize and manipulate independent variables.

    B. recognize and record independent variables.

    C. recognize and manipulate dependent variables.

    D. recognize and record dependent variables.

25. Since ancient times, people have been entranced with bird flight. What is the key to bird flight?

    A. Bird wings are a particular shape and composition.

    B. Birds flap their wings quickly enough to propel themselves.

    C. Birds take advantage of tailwinds.

    D. Birds take advantage of crosswinds.

26. Laboratory researchers have classified fungi as distinct from plants because the cell walls of fungi

    A. contain chitin.

    B. contain yeast.

    C. are more solid.

    D. are less solid.

27. In a fission reactor, "heavy water" is used to

    A. terminate fission reactions.

    B. slow down neutrons and moderate reactions.

    C. rehydrate the chemicals.

    D. initiate a chain reaction.

28. The transfer of heat by electromagnetic waves is called

    A. conduction.

    B. convection.

    C. phase change.

    D. radiation.

29. When heat is added to most solids, they expand. Why is this the case?

    A. The molecules get bigger.

    B. The faster molecular motion leads to greater distance between the molecules.

    C. The molecules develop greater repelling electric forces.

    D. The molecules form a more rigid structure.

30. The force of gravity on earth causes all bodies in free fall to

    A. fall at the same speed.

    B. accelerate at the same rate.

    C. reach the same terminal velocity.

    D. move in the same direction.

31. Sound waves are produced by

    A. pitch.

    B. noise.

    C. vibrations.

    D. sonar.

32. Resistance is measured in units called

    A. watts.

    B. volts.

    C. ohm.

    D. current.

33. Sound can be transmitted in all of the following *except*

    A. air.

    B. water.

    C. diamond.

    D. a vacuum.

34. As a train approaches, the whistle sounds

    A. higher, because it has a higher apparent frequency.

    B. lower, because it has a lower apparent frequency.

    C. higher, because it has a lower apparent frequency.

    D. lower, because it has a higher apparent frequency.

35. The speed of light is different in different materials. This is responsible for

    A. interference.

    B. refraction.

    C. reflection.

    D. relativity.

36. A converging lens produces a real image _____

A. always.

B. never.

C. when the object is within one focal length of the lens.

D. when the object is further than one focal length from the lens.

37. The electromagnetic radiation with the longest wave length is _____

A. radio waves.

B. red light.

C. X-rays.

D. ultraviolet light.

38. Under a 440 power microscope, an object with diameter 0.1 millimeter appears to have diameter

A. 4.4 millimeters.

B. 44 millimeters.

C. 440 millimeters.

D. 4400 millimeters.

39. To separate blood into blood cells and plasma involves the process of

A. electrophoresis.

B. centrifugation.

C. spectrophotometry.

D. chromatography.

40. Experiments may be done with any of the following animals except

A. birds.

B. invertebrates.

C. lower order life.

D. frogs.

41. For her first project of the year, a student is designing a science experiment to test the effects of light and water on plant growth. You should recommend that she _____

A. manipulate the temperature also.

B. manipulate the water pH also.

C. determine the relationship between light and water unrelated to plant growth.

D. omit either water or light as a variable.

42. In a laboratory report, what is the abstract?

A. The abstract is a summary of the report, and is the first section of the report.

B. The abstract is a summary of the report, and is the last section of the report.

C. The abstract is predictions for future experiments, and is the first section of the report.

D. The abstract is predictions for future experiments, and is the last section of the report.

GENERAL SCIENCE

43. What is the scientific method?

A. It is the process of doing an experiment and writing a laboratory report.

B. It is the process of using open inquiry and repeatable results to establish theories.

C. It is the process of reinforcing scientific principles by confirming results.

D. It is the process of recording data and observations.

44. Identify the control in the following experiment: A student had four corn plants and was measuring photosynthetic rate (by measuring growth mass). Half of the plants were exposed to full (constant) sunlight, and the other half were kept in 50% (constant) sunlight.

A. The control is a set of plants grown in full (constant) sunlight.

B. The control is a set of plants grown in 50% (constant) sunlight.

C. The control is a set of plants grown in the dark.

D. The control is a set of plants grown in a mixture of natural levels of sunlight.

45. In an experiment measuring the growth of bacteria at different temperatures, what is the independent variable?

A. Number of bacteria.

B. Growth rate of bacteria.

C. Temperature.

D. Light intensity.

46. A scientific law _____

A. proves scientific accuracy.

B. may never be broken.

C. may be revised in light of new data.

D. is the result of one excellent experiment.

47. Which is the correct order of methodology?

1. **collecting data**
2. **planning a controlled experiment**
3. **drawing a conclusion**
4. **hypothesizing a result**
5. **re-visiting a hypothesis to answer question**

A. 1,2,3,4,5

B. 4,2,1,3,5

C. 4,5,1,3,2

D. 1,3,4,5,2

48. Which is the most desirable tool to use to heat substances in a middle school laboratory?

A. Alcohol burner.

B. Freestanding gas burner.

C. Bunsen burner.

D. Hot plate.

49. Newton's Laws are taught in science classes because _____

A. they are the correct analysis of inertia, gravity, and forces.

B. they are a close approximation to correct physics, for usual Earth conditions.

C. they accurately incorporate Relativity into studies of forces.

D. Newton was a well-respected scientist in his time.

50. Which of the following is most accurate?

A. Mass is always constant; Weight may vary by location.

B. Mass and Weight are both always constant.

C. Weight is always constant; Mass may vary by location.

D. Mass and Weight may both vary by location.

51. Chemicals should be stored

A. in the principal's office.

B. in a dark room.

C. in an off-site research facility.

D. according to their reactivity with other substances.

52. Which of the following is the worst choice for a school laboratory activity?

A. A genetics experiment tracking the fur color of mice.

B. Dissection of a preserved fetal pig.

C. Measurement of goldfish respiration rate at different temperatures.

D. Pithing a frog to watch the circulatory system.

53. Who should be notified in the case of a serious chemical spill?

A. The custodian.

B. The fire department or other municipal authority.

C. The science department chair.

D. The School Board.

54. A scientist exposes mice to cigarette smoke, and notes that their lungs develop tumors. Mice that were not exposed to the smoke do not develop as many tumors. Which of the following conclusions may be drawn from these results?

    I.   Cigarette smoke causes lung tumors.
    II.   Cigarette smoke exposure has a positive correlation with lung tumors in mice.
    III.   Some mice are predisposed to develop lung tumors.
    IV.   Mice are often a good model for humans in scientific research.

A. I and II only.

B. II only.

C. I , II, and III only.

D. II and IV only.

55. In which situation would a science teacher be legally liable?

A The teacher leaves the classroom for a telephone call and a student slips and injures him/herself.

B. A student removes his/her goggles and gets acid in his/her eye.

C. A faulty gas line in the classroom causes a fire.

D. A student cuts him/herself with a dissection scalpel.

56. Which of these is the best example of 'negligence'?

A. A teacher fails to give oral instructio to those with reading disabilities.

B. A teacher fails to exercise ordinary care to ensure safety in the classroom.

C. A teacher displays inability to supervise a large group of students

D. A teacher reasonably anticipates tha an event may occur, and plans accordingly.

57. Which item should always be used wh handling glassware?

A. Tongs.

B. Safety goggles.

C. Gloves.

D. Buret stand.

58. Which of the following is *not* a necessa characteristic of living things?

A. Movement.

B. Reduction of local entropy.

C. Ability to cause local energy form changes.

D. Reproduction.

59. **What are the most significant and prevalent elements in the biosphere?**

    A. Carbon, Hydrogen, Oxygen, Nitrogen, Phosphorus.

    B. Carbon, Hydrogen, Sodium, Iron, Calcium.

    C. Carbon, Oxygen, Sulfur, Manganese, Iron.

    D. Carbon, Hydrogen, Oxygen, Nickel, Sodium, Nitrogen.

60. **All of the following measure energy *except* for _____**

    A. joules.

    B. calories.

    C. watts.

    D. ergs.

61. **Identify the correct sequence of organization of living things from lower to higher order:**

    A. Cell, Organelle, Organ, Tissue, System, Organism.

    B. Cell, Tissue, Organ, Organelle, System, Organism.

    C. Organelle, Cell, Tissue, Organ, System, Organism.

    D. Organelle, Tissue, Cell, Organ, System, Organism.

62. **Which kingdom is comprised of organisms made of one cell with no nuclear membrane?**

    A. Monera.

    B. Protista.

    C. Fungi.

    D. Algae.

63. **Which of the following is found in the least abundance in organic molecules?**

    A. Phosphorus.

    B. Potassium.

    C. Carbon.

    D. Oxygen.

64. **Catalysts assist reactions by**

    A. lowering effective activation energy.

    B. maintaining precise pH levels.

    C. keeping systems at equilibrium.

    D. adjusting reaction speed.

65. **Accepted procedures for preparing solutions should be made with**

    A. alcohol.

    B. hydrochloric acid.

    C. distilled water.

    D. tap water.

66. Enzymes speed up reactions by

    A. utilizing ATP.

    B. lowering pH, allowing reaction speed to increase.

    C. increasing volume of substrate.

    D. lowering energy of activation.

67. When you step out of the shower, the floor feels colder on your feet than the bathmat. Which of the following is the correct explanation for this phenomenon?

    A. The floor is colder than the bathmat.

    B. Your feet have a chemical reaction with the floor, but not the bathmat.

    C. Heat is conducted more easily into the floor.

    D. Water is absorbed from your feet into the bathmat.

68. Which of the following is *not* considered ethical behavior for a scientist?

    A. Using unpublished data and citing the source.

    B. Publishing data before other scientists have had a chance to replicate results.

    C. Collaborating with other scientists from different laboratories.

    D. Publishing work with an incomplete list of citations.

69. The chemical equation for water formation is: $2H_2 + O_2 \rightarrow 2H_2O$. Which of the following is an *incorrect* interpretation of this equation?

    A. Two moles of hydrogen gas and one mole of oxygen gas combine to make two moles of water.

    B. Two grams of hydrogen gas and one gram of oxygen gas combine to make two grams of water.

    C. Two molecules of hydrogen gas and one molecule of oxygen gas combine to make two molecules of water.

    D. Four atoms of hydrogen (combined a diatomic gas) and two atoms of oxygen (combined as a diatomic gas) combine to make two molecules of water.

70. Energy is measured with the same unit as _____

    A. force.

    B. momentum.

    C. work.

    D. power.

1. If the volume of a confined gas is increased, what happens to the pressure of the gas? You may assume that the gas behaves ideally, and that temperature and number of gas molecules remain constant.

   A. The pressure increases.

   B. The pressure decreases.

   C. The pressure stays the same.

   D. There is not enough information given to answer this question.

2. A product of anaerobic respiration in animals is _____

   A. carbon dioxide.

   B. lactic acid.

   C. oxygen.

   D. sodium chloride

3. A Newton is fundamentally a measure of

   A. force.

   B. momentum.

   C. energy.

   D. gravity.

74. Which change does *not* affect enzyme rate?

   A. Increase the temperature.

   B. Add more substrate.

   C. Adjust the pH.

   D. Use a larger cell.

75. Which of the following types of rock are made from magma?

   A. Fossils

   B. Sedimentary

   C. Metamorphic

   D. Igneous

76. Which of the following is *not* an acceptable way for a student to acknowledge sources in a laboratory report?

   A. The student tells his/her teacher what sources s/he used to write the report.

   B. The student uses footnotes in the text, with sources cited, but not in correct MLA format.

   C. The student uses endnotes in the text, with sources cited, in correct MLA format.

   D. The student attaches a separate bibliography, noting each use of sources.

77. **Animals with a notochord or backbone are in the phylum**

    A. arthropoda.

    B. chordata.

    C. mollusca.

    D. mammalia.

78. **Which of the following is a correct explanation for scientific 'evolution'?**

    A. Giraffes need to reach higher for leaves to eat, so their necks stretch. The giraffe babies are then born with longer necks. Eventually, there are more long-necked giraffes in the population.

    B. Giraffes with longer necks are able to reach more leaves, so they eat more and have more babies than other giraffes. Eventually, there are more long-necked giraffes in the population.

    C. Giraffes want to reach higher for leaves to eat, so they release enzymes into their bloodstream, which in turn causes fetal development of longer-necked giraffes. Eventually, there are more long-necked giraffes in the population.

    D. Giraffes with long necks are more attractive to other giraffes, so they get the best mating partners and have more babies. Eventually, there are more long-necked giraffes in the population.

79. **Which of the following is a correct definition for 'chemical equilibrium'?**

    A. Chemical equilibrium is when the forward and backward reaction rates are equal. The reaction may continue to proceed forward and backward.

    B. Chemical equilibrium is when the forward and backward reaction rates are equal, and equal to zero. The reaction does not continue.

    C. Chemical equilibrium is when there are equal quantities of reactants and products.

    D. Chemical equilibrium is when acids and bases neutralize each other full

80. **Which of the following data sets is properly represented by a bar graph?**

    A. Number of people choosing to buy cars, vs. Color of car bought.

    B. Number of people choosing to buy cars, vs. Age of car customer.

    C. Number of people choosing to buy cars, vs. Distance from car lot to customer home.

    D. Number of people choosing to buy cars, vs. Time since last car purcha

81. In a science experiment, a student needs to dispense very small measured amounts of liquid into a well-mixed solution. Which of the following is the best choice for his/her equipment to use?

A. Buret with Buret Stand, Stir-plate, Stirring Rod, Beaker.

B. Buret with Buret Stand, Stir-plate, Beaker.

C. Volumetric Flask, Dropper, Graduated Cylinder, Stirring Rod.

D. Beaker, Graduated Cylinder, Stir-plate.

82. A laboratory balance is most appropriately used to measure the mass of which of the following?

A. Seven paper clips.

B. Three oranges.

C. Two hundred cells.

D. One student's elbow.

83. All of the following are measured in units of length, *except* for:

A. Perimeter.

B. Distance.

C. Radius.

D. Area.

84. What is specific gravity?

A. The mass of an object.

B. The ratio of the density of a substance to the density of water.

C. Density.

D. The pull of the earth's gravity on an object.

85. What is the most accurate description of the Water Cycle?

A. Rain comes from clouds, filling the ocean. The water then evaporates and becomes clouds again.

B. Water circulates from rivers into groundwater and back, while water vapor circulates in the atmosphere.

C. Water is conserved except for chemical or nuclear reactions, and any drop of water could circulate through clouds, rain, ground-water, and surface-water.

D. Weather systems cause chemical reactions to break water into its atoms.

86. The scientific name *Canis familiaris* refers to the animal's _____

A. kingdom and phylum.

B. genus and species.

C. class and species.

D. type and family.

87. Members of the same animal species

A. look identical.

B. never adapt differently.

C. are able to reproduce with one another.

D. are found in the same location.

88. Which of the following is/are true about scientists?

   I.   Scientists usually work alone.

   II.   Scientists usually work with other scientists.

   III. Scientists achieve more prestige from new discoveries than from replicating established results.

   IV. Scientists keep records of their own work, but do not publish it for outside review.

A. I and IV only.

B. II only.

C. II and III only.

D. I and IV only.

89. What is necessary for ion diffusion to occur spontaneously?

A. Carrier proteins.

B. Energy from an outside source.

C. A concentration gradient.

D. Cell flagellae.

90. All of the following are considered Newton's Laws *except* for:

A. An object in motion will continue in motion unless acted upon by an outside force.

B. For every action force, there is an equal and opposite reaction force.

C. Nature abhors a vacuum.

D. Mass can be considered the ratio of force to acceleration.

91. A cup of hot liquid and a cup of cold liquid are both sitting in a room at comfortable room temperature and humidity. Both cups are thin plastic. Which of the following is a true statement?

A. There will be fog on the outside of the hot liquid cup, and also fog on the outside of the cold liquid cup.

B. There will be fog on the outside of the hot liquid cup, but not on the cold liquid cup.

C. There will be fog on the outside of the cold liquid cup, but not on the hot liquid cup.

D. There will not be fog on the outside either cup.

92. A ball rolls down a smooth hill. You may ignore air resistance. Which of the following is a true statement?

A. The ball has more energy at the start of its descent than just before it hits the bottom of the hill, because it is higher up at the beginning.

B. The ball has less energy at the start of its descent than just before it hits the bottom of the hill, because it is moving more quickly at the end.

C. The ball has the same energy throughout its descent, because positional energy is converted to energy of motion.

D. The ball has the same energy throughout its descent, because a single object (such as a ball) cannot gain or lose energy.

93. A long silver bar has a temperature of 50 degrees Celsius at one end and 0 degrees Celsius at the other end. The bar will reach thermal equilibrium (barring outside influence) by the process of heat _____

A. conduction.

B. convection.

C. radiation.

D. phase change.

94. _____ are cracks in the plates of the earth's crust, along which the plates move.

A. Faults.

B. Ridges.

C. Earthquakes.

D. Volcanoes.

95. Fossils are usually found in _____ rock.

A. igneous.

B. sedimentary.

C. metamorphic.

D. cumulus.

96. Which of the following is *not* a common type of acid in 'acid rain' or acidified surface water?

A. Nitric acid.

B. Sulfuric acid.

C. Carbonic acid.

D. Hydrofluoric acid.

97. Which of the following is *not* true about phase change in matter?

   A. Solid water and liquid ice can coexist at water's freezing point.

   B. At 7 degrees Celsius, water is always in liquid phase.

   C. Matter changes phase when enough energy is gained or lost.

   D. Different phases of matter are characterized by differences in molecular motion.

98. Which of the following is the longest (largest) unit of geological time?

   A. Solar Year.

   B. Epoch.

   C. Period.

   D. Era.

99. Extensive use of antibacterial soap has been found to increase the virulence of certain infections in hospitals. Which of the following might be an explanation for this phenomenon?

   A. Antibacterial soaps do not kill viruses.

   B. Antibacterial soaps do not incorporate the same antibiotics used as medicine.

   C. Antibacterial soaps kill a lot of bacteria, and only the hardiest ones survive to reproduce.

   D. Antibacterial soaps can be very drying to the skin.

100. Which of the following is a correct explanation for astronaut 'weightlessness'?

   A. Astronauts continue to feel the pull of gravity in space, but they are so far from planets that the force is small.

   B. Astronauts continue to feel the pull of gravity in space, but spacecraft have such powerful engines that those forces dominate, reducing effective weight.

   C. Astronauts do not feel the pull of gravity in space, because space is a vacuum.

   D. Astronauts do not feel the pull of gravity in space, because black hole forces dominate the force field, reducing their masses.

101. The theory of 'sea floor spreading' explains _____

   A. the shapes of the continents.

   B. how continents collide.

   C. how continents move apart.

   D. how continents sink to become part the ocean floor.

102. Which of the following animals are most likely to live in a tropical rain forest?

   A. Reindeer.

   B. Monkeys.

   C. Puffins.

   D. Bears.

103. Which of the following is *not* a type of volcano?

A. Shield Volcanoes.

B. Composite Volcanoes.

C. Stratus Volcanoes.

D. Cinder Cone Volcanoes.

04. Which of the following is *not* a property of metalloids?

A. Metalloids are solids at standard temperature and pressure.

B. Metalloids can conduct electricity to a limited extent.

C. Metalloids are found in groups 13 through 17.

D. Metalloids all favor ionic bonding.

05. Which of these is a true statement about loamy soil?

A. Loamy soil is gritty and porous.

B. Loamy soil is smooth and a good barrier to water.

C. Loamy soil is hostile to microorganisms.

D. Loamy soil is velvety and clumpy.

106. Lithification refers to the process by which unconsolidated sediments are transformed into _____

A. metamorphic rocks.

B. sedimentary rocks.

C. igneous rocks.

D. lithium oxide.

107. Igneous rocks can be classified according to which of the following?

A. Texture.

B. Composition.

C. Formation process.

D. All of the above.

108. Which of the following is the most accurate definition of a nonrenewable resource?

A. A nonrenewable resource is never replaced once used.

B. A nonrenewable resource is replaced on a timescale that is very long relative to human life-spans.

C. A nonrenewable resource is a resource that can only be manufactured by humans.

D. A nonrenewable resource is a species that has already become extinct.

109. The theory of 'continental drift' is supported by which of the following?

   A. The way the shapes of South America and Europe fit together.

   B. The way the shapes of Europe and Asia fit together.

   C. The way the shapes of South America and Africa fit together.

   D. The way the shapes of North America and Antarctica fit together.

110. When water falls to a cave floor and evaporates, it may deposit calcium carbonate. This process leads to the formation of which of the following?

   A. Stalactites.

   B. Stalagmites.

   C. Fault lines.

   D. Sedimentary rocks.

111. A child has type O blood. Her father has type A blood, and her mother has type B blood. What are the genotypes of the father and mother, respectively?

   A. AO and BO.

   B. AA and AB.

   C. OO and BO.

   D. AO and BB.

112. Which of the following is the best definition for 'meteorite'?

   A. A meteorite is a mineral composed mica and feldspar.

   B. A meteorite is material from outer space, that has struck the earth's surface.

   C. A meteorite is an element that has properties of both metals and nonmetals.

   D. A meteorite is a very small unit of length measurement.

113. A white flower is crossed with a red flower. Which of the following is a sig of incomplete dominance?

   A. Pink flowers.

   B. Red flowers.

   C. White flowers.

   D. No flowers.

114. What is the source for most of the United States' drinking water?

   A. Desalinated ocean water.

   B. Surface water (lakes, streams, mountain runoff).

   C. Rainfall into municipal reservoirs.

   D. Groundwater.

115. Which is the correct sequence of insect development?

    A. Egg, pupa, larva, adult.

    B. Egg, larva, pupa, adult.

    C. Egg, adult, larva, pupa.

    D. Pupa, egg, larva, adult.

16. A wrasse (fish) cleans the teeth of other fish by eating away plaque. This is an example of _____ between the fish.

    A. parasitism.

    B. symbiosis (mutualism).

    C. competition.

    D. predation.

17. What is the main obstacle to using nuclear fusion for obtaining electricity?

    A. Nuclear fusion produces much more pollution than nuclear fission.

    B. There is no obstacle; most power plants us nuclear fusion today.

    C. Nuclear fusion requires very high temperature and activation energy.

    D. The fuel for nuclear fusion is extremely expensive.

118. Which of the following is a true statement about radiation exposure and air travel?

    A. Air travel exposes humans to radiation, but the level is not significant for most people.

    B. Air travel exposes humans to so much radiation that it is recommended as a method of cancer treatment.

    C. Air travel does not expose humans to radiation.

    D. Air travel may or may not expose humans to radiation, but it has not yet been determined.

119. Which process(es) result(s) in a haploid chromosome number?

    A. Mitosis.

    B. Meiosis.

    C. Both mitosis and meiosis.

    D. Neither mitosis nor meiosis.

120. Which of the following is *not* a member of Kingdom Fungi?

    A. Mold.

    B. Blue-green algae.

    C. Mildew.

    D. Mushrooms.

121. Which of the following organisms use spores to reproduce?

   A. Fish.

   B. Flowering plants.

   C. Conifers.

   D. Ferns.

122. What is the main difference between the 'condensation hypothesis' and the 'tidal hypothesis' for the origin of the solar system?

   A. The tidal hypothesis can be tested, but the condensation hypothesis cannot.

   B. The tidal hypothesis proposes a near collision of two stars pulling on each other, but the condensation hypothesis proposes condensation of rotating clouds of dust and gas.

   C. The tidal hypothesis explains how tides began on planets such as Earth, but the condensation hypothesis explains how water vapor became liquid on Earth.

   D. The tidal hypothesis is based on Aristotelian physics, but the condensation hypothesis is based on Newtonian mechanics.

123. Which of the following units is _not_ a measure of distance?

   A. AU (astronomical unit).

   B. Light year.

   C. Parsec.

   D. Lunar year.

124. The salinity of ocean water is closest to _____ .

   A. 0.035 %

   B. 0.35 %

   C. 3.5 %

   D. 35 %

125. Which of the following will not change in a chemical reaction?

   A. Number of moles of products.

   B. Atomic number of one of the reactants.

   C. Mass (in grams) of one of the reactants.

   D. Rate of reaction.

.	B	21.	C	41.	D	61.	C	81.	B	101.	C	121.	D
2.	A	22.	B	42.	A	62.	A	82.	A	102.	B	122.	B
3.	A	23.	A	43.	B	63.	B	83.	D	103.	C	123.	D
4.	C	24.	A	44.	A	64.	A	84.	B	104.	D	124.	C
5.	B	25.	A	45.	C	65.	C	85.	C	105.	D	125.	B
6.	C	26.	A	46.	C	66.	D	86.	B	106.	B		
7.	D	27.	B	47.	B	67.	C	87.	C	107.	D		
8.	C	28.	D	48.	D	68.	D	88.	C	108.	B		
9.	C	29.	B	49.	B	69.	B	89.	C	109.	C		
10.	B	30.	B	50.	A	70.	C	90.	C	110.	B		
11.	A	31.	C	51.	D	71.	B	91.	C	111.	A		
12.	C	32.	C	52.	D	72.	B	92.	C	112.	B		
13.	C	33.	D	53.	B	73.	A	93.	A	113.	A		
14.	B	34.	A	54.	B	74.	D	94.	A	114.	D		
15.	B	35.	B	55.	A	75.	D	95.	B	115.	B		
16.	B	36.	D	56.	B	76.	A	96.	D	116.	B		
17.	A	37.	A	57.	B	77.	B	97.	B	117.	C		
18.	C	38.	B	58.	A	78.	B	98.	D	118.	A		
19.	C	39.	C	59.	A	79.	A	99.	C	119.	B		
20.	D	40.	A	60.	C	80.	A	100.	A	120	B		

GENERAL SCIENCE

1. **After an experiment, the scientist states that s/he believes a change in color is due to a change in pH. This is an example of**

    A. observing.

    B. inferring.

    C. measuring.

    D. classifying.

B. Inferring.

To answer this question, note that the scientist has observed a change in color, and has then made a guess as to its reason. This is an example of inferring. The scientist has not measured or classified in this case. Although s/he has observed [the color change], the explanation of this observation is **inferring (B).**

2. **When is a hypothesis formed?**

    A. Before the data is taken.

    B. After the data is taken.

    C. After the data is analyzed.

    D. While the data is being graphed.

A. Before the data is taken.

A hypothesis is an educated guess, made before undertaking an experiment. The hypothesis is then evaluated based on the observed data. Therefore, the hypothesis must be formed before the data is taken, not during or after the experiment. This is consistent only with **answer (A).**

3. Who determines the laws regarding the use of safety glasses in the classroom?

    A. The state government.

    B. The school site.

    C. The federal government.

    D. The local district.

A. The state government.

Health and safety regulations are set by the state government, and apply to all school districts. Federal regulations may accompany specific federal grants, and local districts or school sites may enact local guidelines that are stricter than the state standards. All schools, however, must abide by safety precautions as set by state government. This is consistent only with **answer (A).**

4. If one inch equals 2.54 centimeters, how many millimeters are in 1.5 feet? (Approximately)

    A. 18

    B. 1800

    C. 460

    D. 4600

C. 460

To solve this problem, note that if one inch is 2.54 centimeters, then 1.5 feet (which is 18 inches), must be (18)(2.54) centimeters, i.e. approximately 46 centimeters. Because there are ten millimeters in a centimeter, this is approximately 460 millimeters:

(1.5 ft) (12 in/ft) (2.54 cm/in) (10 mm/cm) = (1.5) (12) (2.54) (10) mm = 457.2 mm

This is consistent only with **answer (C).**

GENERAL SCIENCE

5. Which of the following instruments measures wind speed?

   A. Barometer.

   B. Anemometer.

   C. Thermometer.

   D. Weather Vane.

B. Anemometer.

An anemometer is a device to measure wind speed, while a barometer measures pressure, a thermometer measures temperature, and a weather vane indicates wind direction. This is consistent only with **answer (B).**

If you chose "barometer," here is an old physics joke to console you:

   A physics teacher asks a student the following question:
   "Suppose you want to find out the height of a building, and the only tool you have is a barometer. How could you find out the height?"
   (The teacher hopes that the student will remember that pressure is inversely proportional to height, and will measure the pressure at the top of the building and then use the data to calculate the height of the building.)
   "Well," says the student, "I could tie a string to the barometer and lower it from the top of the building, and then measure the amount of string required."
   "You could," answers the teacher, "but try to think of a method that uses your physics knowledge from our class."
   "All right," replies the student, "I could drop the barometer from the roof and measure the time it takes to fall, and then use free-fall equations to calculate the height from which it fell."
   "Yes," says the teacher, "but what about using the barometer per se?"
   "Oh," answers the student, "I could find the building superintendent, and offer to exchange the barometer for a set of blueprints, and look up the height!"

6. Sonar works by

    A. timing how long it takes sound to reach a certain speed.

    B. bouncing sound waves between two metal plates.

    C. bouncing sound waves off an object and timing how long it takes for the sound to return.

    D. evaluating the motion and amplitude of sound.

C. Bouncing sound waves off an object and timing how long it takes for the sound to return.

Sonar is used to measure distances. Sound waves are sent out, and the time is measured for the sound to hit an obstacle and bounce back. By using the known speed of sound, observers (or machines) can calculate the distance to the obstacle. This is consistent only with **answer (C).**

7. The measure of the pull of Earth's gravity on an object is called

    A. mass number.

    B. atomic number.

    C. mass.

    D. weight.

D. Weight.

To answer this question, recall that mass number is the total number of protons and neutrons in an atom, atomic number is the number of protons in an atom, and mass is the amount of matter in an object. The only remaining **choice is (D)**, weight, which is correct because weight is the force of gravity on an object.

8. **Which reaction below is a decomposition reaction?**

    A. $HCl + NaOH \rightarrow NaCl + H_2O$

    B. $C + O_2 \rightarrow CO_2$

    C. $2H_2O \rightarrow 2H_2 + O_2$

    D. $CuSO_4 + Fe \rightarrow FeSO_4 + Cu$

C. $2H_2O \rightarrow 2H_2 + O_2$

To answer this question, recall that a decomposition reaction is one in which there are fewer reactants (on the left) than products (on the right). This is consistent only with **answer (C).** Meanwhile, note that answer (A) shows a double-replacement reaction (in which two sets of ions switch bonds), answer (B) shows a synthesis reaction (in which there are fewer products than reactants), and answer (D) shows a single-replacement reaction (in which one substance replaces another in its bond, but the other does not get a new bond).

9. **The Law of Conservation of Energy states that**

    A. there must be the same number of products and reactants in any chemical equation.

    B. objects always fall toward large masses such as planets.

    C. energy is neither created nor destroyed, but may change form.

    D. lights must be turned off when not in use, by state regulation.

C. Energy is neither created nor destroyed, but may change form.

Answer (C) is a summary of the Law of Conservation of Energy (for non-nuclear reactions). In other words, energy can be transformed into various forms such as kinetic, potential, electric, or heat energy, but the total amount of energy remains constant. Answer (A) is untrue, as demonstrated by many synthesis and decomposition reactions. Answers (B) and (D) may be sensible, but they are not relevant in this case. Therefore, the **answer is (C).**

10. Which parts of an atom are located inside the nucleus?

    A. Protons and Electrons.

    B. Protons and Neutrons.

    C. Protons only.

    D. Neutrons only.

B. Protons and Neutrons.

Protons and neutrons are located in the nucleus, while electrons move around outside the nucleus. This is consistent only with **answer (B)**.

11. The elements in the modern Periodic Table are arranged

    A. in numerical order by atomic number.

    B. randomly.

    C. in alphabetical order by chemical symbol.

    D. in numerical order by atomic mass.

A. In numerical order by atomic number.

Although the first periodic tables were arranged by atomic mass, the modern table is arranged by atomic number, i.e. the number of protons in each element. (This allows the element list to be complete and unique.) The elements are not arranged either randomly or in alphabetical order. The answer to this question is **therefore (A)**.

12. Carbon bonds with hydrogen by

   A. ionic bonding.

   B. non-polar covalent bonding.

   C. polar covalent bonding.

   D. strong nuclear force.

C. Polar covalent bonding.

Each carbon atom contains four valence electrons, while each hydrogen atom contains one valence electron. A carbon atom can bond with one or more hydrogen atoms, such that two electrons are shared in each bond. This is covalent bonding, because the electrons are shared. (In ionic bonding, atoms must gain or lose electrons to form ions. The ions are then electrically attracted in oppositely-charged pairs.) Covalent bonds are always polar when between two non-identical atoms, so this bond must be polar. ("Polar" means that the electrons are shared unequally, forming a pair of partial charges, i.e. poles.) In any case, the strong nuclear force is not relevant to this problem. The answer to this question is **therefore (C).**

13. Vinegar is an example of a

   A. strong acid.

   B. strong base.

   C. weak acid.

   D. weak base.

C. Weak acid.

The main ingredient in vinegar is acetic acid, a weak acid. Vinegar is a useful acid in science classes, because it makes a frothy reaction with bases such as baking soda (e.g. in the quintessential volcano model). Vinegar is not a strong acid, such as hydrochloric acid, because it does not dissociate as fully or cause as much corrosion. It is not a base. Therefore, the **answer is (C)**.

14. Which of the following is not a nucleotide?

    A. Adenine.

    B. Alanine.

    C. Cytosine.

    D. Guanine.

B. Alanine.

Alanine is an amino acid. Adenine, cytosine, guanine, thymine, and uracil are nucleotides. The correct **answer is (B).**

15. When measuring the volume of water in a graduated cylinder, where does one read the measurement?

    A. At the highest point of the liquid.

    B. At the bottom of the meniscus curve.

    C. At the closest mark to the top of the liquid.

    D. At the top of the plastic safety ring.

B. At the bottom of the meniscus curve.

To measure water in glass, you must look at the top surface at eye-level, and ascertain the location of the bottom of the meniscus (the curved surface at the top of the water). The meniscus forms because water molecules adhere to the sides of the glass, which is a slightly stronger force than their cohesion to each other. This leads to a U-shaped top of the liquid column, the bottom of which gives the most accurate volume measurement. (Other liquids have different forces, e.g. mercury in glass, which has a convex meniscus.) This is consistent only with **answer (B).**

        GENERAL SCIENCE

16. **A duck's webbed feet are examples of**

    A. mimicry.

    B. structural adaptation.

    C. protective resemblance.

    D. protective coloration.

B. Structural adaptation.

Ducks (and other aquatic birds) have webbed feet, which makes them more efficient swimmers. This is most likely due to evolutionary patterns where webbed-footed-birds were more successful at feeding and reproducing, and eventually became the majority of aquatic birds. Because the structure of the duck adapted to its environment over generations, this is termed 'structural adaptation'. Mimicry, protective resemblance, and protective coloration refer to other evolutionary mechanisms for survival. The answer to this question is **therefore (B)**.

17. **What cell organelle contains the cell's stored food?**

    A. Vacuoles.

    B. Golgi Apparatus.

    C. Ribosomes.

    D. Lysosomes.

A. Vacuoles.

In a cell, the sub-parts are called organelles. Of these, the vacuoles hold stored food (and water and pigments). The Golgi Apparatus sorts molecules from other parts of the cell; the ribosomes are sites of protein synthesis; the lysosomes contain digestive enzymes. This is consistent only with **answer (A).**

18. The first stage of mitosis is called

    A. telophase.

    B. anaphase.

    C. prophase.

    D. mitophase.

C. Prophase.

In mitosis, the division of somatic cells, prophase is the stage where the cell enters mitosis. The four stages of mitosis, in order, are: prophase, metaphase, anaphase, and telophase. ("Mitophase" is not one of the steps.) During prophase, the cell begins the nonstop process of division. Its chromatin condenses, its nucleolus disappears, the nuclear membrane breaks apart, mitotic spindles form, its cytoskeleton breaks down, and centrioles push the spindles apart. Note that interphase, the stage where chromatin is loose, chromosomes are replicated, and cell metabolism is occurring, is technically not a stage of mitosis; it is a precursor to cell division.

19. The Doppler Effect is associated most closely with which property of waves?

    A. Amplitude.

    B. Wavelength.

    C. Frequency.

    D. Intensity.

C. Frequency.

The Doppler Effect accounts for an apparent increase in frequency when a wave source moves toward a wave receiver or apparent decrease in frequency when a wave source moves away from a wave receiver. (Note that the receiver could also be moving toward or away from the source.) As the wave fronts are released, motion toward the receiver mimics more frequent wave fronts, while motion away from the receiver mimics less frequent wave fronts. Meanwhile, the amplitude, wavelength, and intensity of the wave are not as relevant to this process (although moving closer to a wave source makes it seem more intense). The **answer to this question is therefore (C)**.

20. **Viruses are responsible for many human diseases including all of the following *except***

    A. influenza.

    B. A.I.D.S.

    C. the common cold.

    D. strep throat.

D. Strep throat.

Influenza, A.I.D.S., and the "common cold" (rhinovirus infection), are all caused by viruses. (This is the reason that doctors should not be pressured to prescribe antibiotics for colds or 'flu—i.e. they will not be effective since the infections are not bacterial.) Strep throat (properly called 'streptococcal throat' and caused by streptococcus bacteria) is not a virus, but a bacterial infection. Thus, the **answer is (D)**.

21. **A series of experiments on pea plants formed by _____ showed that two invisible markers existed for each trait, and one marker dominated the other.**

    A. Pasteur.

    B. Watson and Crick.

    C. Mendel.

    D. Mendeleev.

C. Mendel.

Gregor Mendel was a ninteenth-century Austrian botanist, who derived "laws" governing inherited traits. His work led to the understanding of dominant and recessive traits, carried by biological markers. Mendel cross-bred different kinds of pea plants with varying features and observed the resulting new plants. He showed that genetic characteristics are not passed identically from one generation to the next. (Pasteur, Watson, Crick, and Mendeleev were other scientists with different specialties.) This is consistent only with **answer (C)**.

22. **Formaldehyde should not be used in school laboratories for the following reason:**

    A. it smells unpleasant.

    B. it is a known carcinogen.

    C. it is expensive to obtain.

    D. it is an explosive.

B. It is a known carcinogen.

Formaldehyde is a known carcinogen, so it is too dangerous for use in schools. In general, teachers should not use carcinogens in school laboratories. Although formaldehyde also smells unpleasant, a smell alone is not a definitive marker of danger. For example, many people find the smell of vinegar to be unpleasant, but vinegar is considered a very safe classroom/laboratory chemical. Furthermore, some odorless materials are toxic. Formaldehyde is neither particularly expensive nor explosive. Thus, the **answer is (B)**.

23. **Amino acids are carried to the ribosome in protein synthesis by:**

    A. transfer RNA (tRNA).

    B. messenger RNA (mRNA).

    C. ribosomal RNA (rRNA).

    D. transformation RNA (trRNA).

A. Transfer RNA (tRNA).

The job of tRNA is to carry and position amino acids to/on the ribosomes. mRNA copies DNA code and brings it to the ribosomes; rRNA is in the ribosome itself. There is no such thing as trRNA. Thus, the **answer is (A)**.

24. **When designing a scientific experiment, a student considers all the factors that may influence the results. The process goal is to**

    A. recognize and manipulate independent variables.

    B. recognize and record independent variables.

    C. recognize and manipulate dependent variables.

    D. recognize and record dependent variables.

A. Recognize and manipulate independent variables.

When a student designs a scientific experiment, s/he must decide what to measure, and what independent variables will play a role in the experiment. S/he must determine how to manipulate these independent variables to refine his/her procedure and to prepare for meaningful observations. Although s/he will eventually record dependent variables (D), this does not take place during the experimental design phase. Although the student will likely recognize and record the independent variables (B), this is not the process goal, but a helpful step in manipulating the variables. It is unlikely that the student will manipulate dependent variables directly in his/her experiment (C), or the data would be suspect. Thus, the **answer is (A)**.

25. **Since ancient times, people have been entranced with bird flight. What is the key to bird flight?**

    A. Bird wings are a particular shape and composition.

    B. Birds flap their wings quickly enough to propel themselves.

    C. Birds take advantage of tailwinds.

    D. Birds take advantage of crosswinds.

A. Bird wings are a particular shape.

Bird wings are shaped for wide area, and their bones are very light. This creates a large surface-area-to-mass ratio, enabling birds to glide in air. Birds do flap their wings and float on winds, but none of these is the main reason for their flight ability. Thus, the **answer is (A)**.

26. Laboratory researchers have classified fungi as distinct from plants because the cell walls of fungi

    A. contain chitin.

    B. contain yeast.

    C. are more solid.

    D. are less solid.

A. Contain chitin.

Kingdom Fungi consists of organisms that are eukaryotic, multicellular, absorptive consumers. They have a chitin cell wall, which is the only universally present feature in fungi that is never present in plants. Thus, the **answer is (A)**.

27. In a fission reactor, "heavy water" is used to

    A. terminate fission reactions.

    B. slow down neutrons and moderate reactions.

    C. rehydrate the chemicals.

    D. initiate a chain reaction.

B. Slow down neutrons and moderate reactions.

"Heavy water" is used in a nuclear [fission] reactor to slow down neutrons, controlling and moderating the nuclear reactions. It does not terminate the reaction, and it does not initiate the reaction. Also, although the reactor takes advantage of water's other properties (e.g. high specific heat for cooling), the water does not "rehydrate" the chemicals. Therefore, the **answer is (B)**.

28. The transfer of heat by electromagnetic waves is called

    A. conduction.

    B. convection.

    C. phase change.

    D. radiation.

D. Radiation.

Heat transfer via electromagnetic waves (which can occur even in a vacuum) is called radiation. (Heat can also be transferred by direct contact (conduction), by fluid current (convection), and by matter changing phase, but these are not relevant here.) The answer to this question is **therefore (D)**.

29. When heat is added to most solids, they expand. Why is this the case?

    A. The molecules get bigger.

    B. The faster molecular motion leads to greater distance between the molecules.

    C. The molecules develop greater repelling electric forces.

    D. The molecules form a more rigid structure.

B. The faster molecular motion leads to greater distance between the molecules.

The atomic theory of matter states that matter is made up of tiny, rapidly moving particles. These particles move more quickly when warmer, because temperature is a measure of average kinetic energy of the particles. Warmer molecules therefore move further away from each other, with enough energy to separate from each other more often and for greater distances. The individual molecules do not get bigger, by conservation of mass, eliminating answer (A). The molecules do not develop greater repelling electric forces, eliminating answer (C). Occasionally, molecules form a more rigid structure when becoming colder and freezing (such as water)—but this gives rise to the exceptions to heat expansion, so it is not relevant here, eliminating answer (D). Therefore, the **answer is (B)**.

30. The force of gravity on earth causes all bodies in free fall to

    A. fall at the same speed.

    B. accelerate at the same rate.

    C. reach the same terminal velocity.

    D. move in the same direction.

B. Accelerate at the same rate.

Gravity causes approximately the same acceleration on all falling bodies close to earth's surface. (It is only "approximately" because there are very small variations in the strength of earth's gravitational field.) More massive bodies continue to accelerate at this rate for longer, before their air resistance is great enough to cause terminal velocity, so answers (A) and (C) are eliminated. Bodies on different parts of the planet move in different directions (always toward the center of mass of earth), so answer (D) is eliminated. Thus, the **answer is (B)**.

31. Sound waves are produced by

    A. pitch.

    B. noise.

    C. vibrations.

    D. sonar.

C. Vibrations.

Sound waves are produced by a vibrating body. The vibrating object moves forward and compresses the air in front of it, then reverses direction so that the pressure on the air is lessened and expansion of the air molecules occurs. The vibrating air molecules move back and forth parallel to the direction of motion of the wave as they pass the energy from adjacent air molecules closer to the source to air molecules farther away from the source. Therefore, the **answer is (C)**.

32. Resistance is measured in units called

    A. watts.

    B. volts.

    C. ohms.

    D. current.

C. Ohms.

A watt is a unit of energy. Potential difference is measured in a unit called the volt. Current is the number of electrons per second that flow past a point in a circuit. An ohm is the unit for resistance. The correct **answer is (C).**

33. Sound can be transmitted in all of the following *except*

    A. air.

    B. water.

    C. diamond.

    D. a vacuum.

D. A vacuum.

Sound, a longitudinal wave, is transmitted by vibrations of molecules. Therefore, it can be transmitted through any gas, liquid, or solid. However, it cannot be transmitted through a vacuum, because there are no particles present to vibrate and bump into their adjacent particles to transmit the waves. This is consistent only with **answer (D).** (It is interesting also to note that sound is actually faster in solids and liquids than in air.)

34. As a train approaches, the whistle sounds

    A. higher, because it has a higher apparent frequency.

    B. lower, because it has a lower apparent frequency.

    C. higher, because it has a lower apparent frequency.

    D. lower, because it has a higher apparent frequency.

A. Higher, because it has a higher apparent frequency.

By the Doppler effect, when a source of sound is moving toward an observer, the wave fronts are released closer together, i.e. with a greater apparent frequency. Higher frequency sounds are higher in pitch. This is consistent only with **answer (A)**.

35. The speed of light is different in different materials. This is responsible for

    A. interference.

    B. refraction.

    C. reflection.

    D. relativity.

B. Refraction.

Refraction (B) is the bending of light because it hits a material at an angle wherein it has a different speed. (This is analogous to a cart rolling on a smooth road. If it hits a rough patch at an angle, the wheel on the rough patch slows down first, leading to a change in direction.) Interference (A) is when light waves interfere with each other to form brighter or dimmer patterns; reflection (C) is when light bounces off a surface; relativity (D) is a general topic related to light speed and its implications, but not specifically indicated here. Therefore, the **answer is (B)**.

36. A converging lens produces a real image _____

    A. always.

    B. never.

    C. when the object is within one focal length of the lens.

    D. when the object is further than one focal length from the lens.

D. When the object is further than one focal length from the lens.

A converging lens produces a real image whenever the object is far enough from the lens (outside one focal length) so that the rays of light from the object can hit the lens and be focused into a real image on the other side of the lens. When the object is closer than one focal length from the lens, rays of light do not converge on the other side; they diverge. This means that only a virtual image can be formed, i.e. the theoretical place where those diverging rays would have converged if they had originated behind the object. Thus, the correct **answer is (D)**.

37. The electromagnetic radiation with the longest wave length is _____

    A. radio waves.

    B. red light.

    C. X-rays.

    D. ultraviolet light.

A. Radio waves.

As one can see on a diagram of the electromagnetic spectrum, radio waves have longer wave lengths (and smaller frequencies) than visible light, which in turn has longer wave lengths than ultraviolet or X-ray radiation. If you did not remember this sequence, you might recall that wave length is inversely proportional to frequency, and that radio waves are considered much less harmful (less energetic, i.e. lower frequency) than ultraviolet or X-ray radiation. The correct answer is **therefore (A)**.

38. Under a 440 power microscope, an object with diameter 0.1 millimeter appears to have diameter _____

    A. 4.4 millimeters.

    B. 44 millimeters.

    C. 440 millimeters.

    D. 4400 millimeters.

B. 44 millimeters.

To answer this question, recall that to calculate a new length, you multiply the original length by the magnification power of the instrument. Therefore, the 0.1 millimeter diameter is multiplied by 440. This equals 44, so the image appears to be 44 millimeters in diameter. You could also reason that since a 440 power microscope is considered a "high power" microscope, you would expect a 0.1 millimeter object to appear a few centimeters long. Therefore, the correct **answer is (B)**.

39. To separate blood into blood cells and plasma involves the process of

    A. electrophoresis.

    B. centrifugation.

    C. spectrophotometry.

    D. chromatography.

C. Centrifugation.

Electrophoresis uses electrical charges of molecules to separate them according to their size. Spectrophotometry uses percent light absorbance to measure a color change, thus giving qualitative data a quantitative value. Chromatography uses the principles of capillarity to separate substances. Centrifugation involves spinning substances at a high speed. The more dense part of a solution will settle to the bottom of the test tube, where the lighter material will stay on top. The **answer is (B)**.

40. Experiments may be done with any of the following animals except

    A. birds.

    B. invertebrates.

    C. lower order life.

    D. frogs.

A. Birds.

No dissections may be performed on living mammalian vertebrates or birds. Lower order life and invertebrates may be used. Biological experiments may be done with all animals except mammalian vertebrates or birds. Therefore the **answer is (A)**.

41. For her first project of the year, a student is designing a science experiment to test the effects of light and water on plant growth. You should recommend that she _____

    A. manipulate the temperature also.

    B. manipulate the water pH also.

    C. determine the relationship between light and water unrelated to plant growth.

    D. omit either water or light as a variable.

D. Omit either water or light as a variable.

As a science teacher for middle-school-aged kids, it is important to reinforce the idea of 'constant' vs. 'variable' in science experiments. At this level, it is wisest to have only one variable examined in each science experiment. (Later, students can hold different variables constant while investigating others.) Therefore it is counterproductive to add in other variables (answers (A) or (B)). It is also irrelevant to determine the light-water interactions aside from plant growth (C). So the only possible **answer is (D)**.

42. In a laboratory report, what is the abstract?

A. The abstract is a summary of the report, and is the first section of the report.

B. The abstract is a summary of the report, and is the last section of the report.

C. The abstract is predictions for future experiments, and is the first section of the report.

D. The abstract is predictions for future experiments, and is the last section of the report.

A. The abstract is a summary of the report, and is the first section of the report.

In a laboratory report, the abstract is the section that summarizes the entire report (often containing one representative sentence from each section). It appears at the very beginning of the report, even before the introduction, often on its own page (instead of a title page). This format is consistent with articles in scientific journals. Therefore, the **answer is (A).**

43. What is the scientific method?

A. It is the process of doing an experiment and writing a laboratory report.

B. It is the process of using open inquiry and repeatable results to establish theories.

C. It is the process of reinforcing scientific principles by confirming results.

D. It is the process of recording data and observations.

B. It is the process of using open inquiry and repeatable results to establish theories.

Scientific research often includes elements from answers (A), (C), and (D), but the basic underlying principle of the scientific method is that people ask questions and do repeatable experiments to answer those questions and develop informed theories of why and how things happen. Therefore, the best **answer is (B).**

44. Identify the control in the following experiment: A student had four corn plants and was measuring photosynthetic rate (by measuring growth mass). Half of the plants were exposed to full (constant) sunlight, and the other half were kept in 50% (constant) sunlight.

    A. The control is a set of plants grown in full (constant) sunlight.

    B. The control is a set of plants grown in 50% (constant) sunlight.

    C. The control is a set of plants grown in the dark.

    D. The control is a set of plants grown in a mixture of natural levels of sunlight.

A. The control is a set of plants grown in full (constant) sunlight.

In this experiment, the goal was to measure how two different amounts of sunlight affected plant growth. The control in any experiment is the 'base case,' or the usual situation without a change in variable. Because the control must be studied alongside the variable, answers (C) and (D) are omitted (because they were not in the experiment). The **better answer of (A) and (B) is (A)**, because usually plants are assumed to have the best growth and their usual growing circumstances in full sunlight. This is particularly true for crops like the corn plants in this question.

45. In an experiment measuring the growth of bacteria at different temperatures, what is the independent variable?

    A. Number of bacteria.

    B. Growth rate of bacteria.

    C. Temperature.

    D. Light intensity.

C. Temperature.

To answer this question, recall that the independent variable in an experiment is the entity that is changed by the scientist, in order to observe the effects (the dependent variable(s)). In this experiment, temperature is changed in order to measure growth of bacteria, so **(C) is the answer**. Note that answer (A) is the dependent variable, and neither (B) nor (D) is directly relevant to the question.

46. A scientific law _____

    A. proves scientific accuracy.

    B. may never be broken.

    C. may be revised in light of new data.

    D. is the result of one excellent experiment.

C. May be revised in light of new data.

A scientific law is the same as a scientific theory, except that it has lasted for longer, and has been supported by more extensive data. Therefore, such a law may be revised in light of new data, and may be broken by that new data. Furthermore, a scientific law is always the result of many experiments, and never 'proves' anything but rather is implied or supported by various results. Therefore, the **answer must be (C).**

47. Which is the correct order of methodology?

    1. collecting data
    2. planning a controlled experiment
    3. drawing a conclusion
    4. hypothesizing a result
    5. re-visiting a hypothesis to answer a question

    A. 1,2,3,4,5

    B. 4,2,1,3,5

    C. 4,5,1,3,2

    D. 1,3,4,5,2

B. 4.2.1.3.5

The correct methodology for the scientific method is first to make a meaningful hypothesis (educated guess), then plan and execute a controlled experiment to test that hypothesis. Using the data collected in that experiment, the scientist then draws conclusions and attempts to answer the original question related to the hypothesis. This is consistent only with **answer (B).**

48. **Which is the most desirable tool to use to heat substances in a middle school laboratory?**

      A. Alcohol burner.

      B. Freestanding gas burner.

      C. Bunsen burner.

      D. Hot plate.

D. Hot plate.

Due to safety considerations, the use of open flame should be minimized, so a Hot Plate is the best choice. Any kind of burner may be used with proper precautions, but it is difficult to maintain a completely safe middle school environment. Therefore, the best **answer is (D)**.

49. **Newton's Laws are taught in science classes because** _____

      A. they are the correct analysis of inertia, gravity, and forces.

      B. they are a close approximation to correct physics, for usual Earth conditions.

      C. they accurately incorporate Relativity into studies of forces.

      D. Newton was a well-respected scientist in his time.

B. They are a close approximation to correct physics, for usual Earth conditions.

Although Newton's Laws are often taught as fully correct for inertia, gravity, and forces, it is important to realize that Einstein's work (and that of others) has indicated that Newton's Laws are reliable only at speeds much lower than that of light. This is reasonable, though, for most middle- and high-school applications. At speeds close to the speed of light, Relativity considerations must be used. Therefore, the only correct **answer is (B)**.

50. Which of the following is most accurate?

    A. Mass is always constant; Weight may vary by location.

    B. Mass and Weight are both always constant.

    C. Weight is always constant; Mass may vary by location.

    D. Mass and Weight may both vary by location.

A. Mass is always constant; Weight may vary by location.

When considering situations exclusive of nuclear reactions, mass is constant (mass, the amount of matter in a system, is conserved). Weight, on the other hand, is the force of gravity on an object, which is subject to change due to changes in the gravitational field and/or the location of the object. Thus, the **best answer is (A)**.

51. Chemicals should be stored _____

    A. in the principal's office.

    B. in a dark room.

    C. in an off-site research facility.

    D. according to their reactivity with other substances.

D. According to their reactivity with other substances.

Chemicals should be stored with other chemicals of similar properties (e.g. acids with other acids), to reduce the potential for either hazardous reactions in the store-room, or mistakes in reagent use. Certainly, chemicals should not be stored in anyone's office, and the light intensity of the room is not very important because light-sensitive chemicals are usually stored in dark containers. In fact, good lighting is desirable in a store-room, so that labels can be read easily. Chemicals may be stored off-site, but that makes their use inconvenient. Therefore, the best **answer is (D)**.

52. Which of the following is the worst choice for a school laboratory activity?

    A. A genetics experiment tracking the fur color of mice.

    B. Dissection of a preserved fetal pig.

    C. Measurement of goldfish respiration rate at different temperatures.

    D. Pithing a frog to watch the circulatory system.

D. Pithing a frog to watch the circulatory system.

While any use of animals (alive or dead) must be done with care to respect ethics and laws, it is possible to perform choices (A), (B), or (C) with due care. (Note that students will need significant assistance and maturity to perform these experiments.) However, modern practice precludes pithing animals (causing partial brain death while allowing some systems to function), as inhumane. Therefore, the answer to this **question is (D)**.

53. Who should be notified in the case of a serious chemical spill?

    A. The custodian.

    B. The fire department or other municipal authority.

    C. The science department chair.

    D. The School Board.

B. The fire department or other municipal authority.

Although the custodian may help to clean up laboratory messes, and the science department chair should be involved in discussions of ways to avoid spills, a serious chemical spill may require action by the fire department or other trained emergency personnel. It is best to be safe by notifying them in case of a serious chemical accident. Therefore, the **best answer is (B)**.

54. A scientist exposes mice to cigarette smoke, and notes that their lungs develop tumors. Mice that were not exposed to the smoke do not develop as many tumors. Which of the following conclusions may be drawn from these results?

     I.   Cigarette smoke causes lung tumors.
     II.   Cigarette smoke exposure has a positive correlation with lung tumors in mice.
     III.   Some mice are predisposed to develop lung tumors.
     IV.   Mice are often a good model for humans in scientific research.

  A. I and II only.

  B. II only.

  C. I , II, and III only.

  D. II and IV only.

B. II only.

Although cigarette smoke has been found to cause lung tumors (and many other problems), this particular experiment shows only that there is a positive correlation between smoke exposure and tumor development in these mice. It may be true that some mice are more likely to develop tumors than others, which is why a control group of identical mice should have been used for comparison. Mice are often used to model human reactions, but this is as much due to their low financial and emotional cost as it is due to their being a "good model" for humans. Therefore, the **answer must be (B)**.

55. In which situation would a science teacher be legally liable?

A. The teacher leaves the classroom for a telephone call and a student slips and injures him/herself.

B. A student removes his/her goggles and gets acid in his/her eye.

C. A faulty gas line in the classroom causes a fire.

D. A student cuts him/herself with a dissection scalpel.

A. The teacher leaves the classroom for a telephone call and a student slips and injures him/herself.

Teachers are required to exercise a "reasonable duty of care" for their students. Accidents may happen (e.g. (D)), or students may make poor decisions (e.g. (B)), or facilities may break down (e.g. (C)). However, the teacher has the responsibility to be present and to do his/her best to create a safe and effective learning environment. Therefore, the **answer is (A)**.

56. Which of these is the best example of 'negligence'?

A. A teacher fails to give oral instructions to those with reading disabilities.

B. A teacher fails to exercise ordinary care to ensure safety in the classroom.

C. A teacher displays inability to supervise a large group of students.

D. A teacher reasonably anticipates that an event may occur, and plans accordingly.

B. A teacher fails to exercise ordinary care to ensure safety in the classroom.

'Negligence' is the failure to "exercise ordinary care" to ensure an appropriate and safe classroom environment. It is best for a teacher to meet all special requirements for disabled students, and to be good at supervising large groups. However, if a teacher can prove that s/he has done a reasonable job to ensure a safe and effective learning environment, then it is unlikely that s/he would be found negligent. Therefore, **the answer is (B)**.

57. Which item should always be used when handling glassware?

    A. Tongs.

    B. Safety goggles.

    C. Gloves.

    D. Buret stand.

B. Safety goggles.

Safety goggles are the single most important piece of safety equipment in the laboratory, and should be used any time a scientist is using glassware, heat, or chemicals. Other equipment (e.g. tongs, gloves, or even a buret stand) has its place for various applications. However, the sine qua non is safety goggles. Therefore, the **answer is (B)**.

58. Which of the following is *not* a necessary characteristic of living things?

    A. Movement.

    B. Reduction of local entropy.

    C. Ability to cause local energy form changes.

    D. Reproduction.

A. Movement.

There are many definitions of "life," but in all cases, a living organism reduces local entropy, changes chemical energy into other forms, and reproduces. Not all living things move, however, so the correct **answer is (A)**.

59. What are the most significant and prevalent elements in the biosphere?

    A. Carbon, Hydrogen, Oxygen, Nitrogen, Phosphorus.

    B. Carbon, Hydrogen, Sodium, Iron, Calcium.

    C. Carbon, Oxygen, Sulfur, Manganese, Iron.

    D. Carbon, Hydrogen, Oxygen, Nickel, Sodium, Nitrogen.

A. Carbon, Hydrogen, Oxygen, Nitrogen, Phosphorus.

Organic matter (and life as we know it) is based on Carbon atoms, bonded to Hydrogen and Oxygen. Nitrogen and Phosphorus are the next most significant elements, followed by Sulfur and then trace nutrients such as Iron, Sodium, Calcium, and others. Therefore, the **answer is (A)**. If you know that the formula for any carbohydrate contains Carbon, Hydrogen, and Oxygen, that will help you narrow the choices to (A) and (D) in any case.

60. All of the following measure energy *except* for _____

    A. joules.

    B. calories.

    C. watts.

    D. ergs.

C. Watts.

Energy units must be dimensionally equivalent to (force)x(length), which equals (mass)x(length squared)/(time squared). Joules, Calories, and Ergs are all metric measures of energy. Joules are the SI units of energy, while Calories are used to allow water to have a Specific Heat of one unit. Ergs are used in the 'cgs' (centimeter-gram-second) system, for smaller quantities. Watts, however, are units of power, i.e. Joules per Second. Therefore, the **answer is (C)**.

61. Identify the correct sequence of organization of living things from lower to higher order:

    A. Cell, Organelle, Organ, Tissue, System, Organism.

    B. Cell, Tissue, Organ, Organelle, System, Organism.

    C. Organelle, Cell, Tissue, Organ, System, Organism.

    D. Organelle, Tissue, Cell, Organ, System, Organism.

C. Organelle, Cell, Tissue, Organ, System, Organism.

Organelles are parts of the cell; cells make up tissue, which makes up organs. Organs work together in systems (e.g. the respiratory system), and the organism is the living thing as a whole. Therefore, the **answer must be (C)**.

62. Which kingdom is comprised of organisms made of one cell with no nuclear membrane?

    A. Monera.

    B. Protista.

    C. Fungi.

    D. Algae.

A. Monera.

To answer this question, first note that algae are not a kingdom of their own. Some algae are in monera, the kingdom that consists of unicellular prokaryotes with no true nucleus. Protista and fungi are both eukaryotic, with true nuclei, and are sometimes multi-cellular. Therefore, the **answer is (A)**.

63. Which of the following is found in the least abundance in organic molecules?

  A. Phosphorus.

  B. Potassium.

  C. Carbon.

  D. Oxygen.

B. Potassium.

Organic molecules consist mainly of Carbon, Hydrogen, and Oxygen, with significant amounts of Nitrogen, Phosphorus, and often Sulfur. Other elements, such as Potassium, are present in much smaller quantities. Therefore, the **answer is (B)**. If you were not aware of this ranking, you might have been able to eliminate Carbon and Oxygen because of their prevalence, in any case.

64. Catalysts assist reactions by _____

  A. lowering effective activation energy.

  B. maintaining precise pH levels.

  C. keeping systems at equilibrium.

  D. adjusting reaction speed.

A. Lowering effective activation energy.

Chemical reactions can be enhanced or accelerated by catalysts, which are present both with reactants and with products. They induce the formation of activated complexes, thereby lowering the effective activation energy—so that less energy is necessary for the reaction to begin. Although this often makes reactions faster, answer (D) is not as good a choice as the more generally applicable **answer (A)**, which is correct.

65. Accepted procedures for preparing solutions should be made with

A. alcohol.

B. hydrochloric acid.

C. distilled water.

D. tap water.

C. Distilled water.

Alcohol and hydrochloric acid should never be used to make solutions unless instructed to do so. All solutions should be made with distilled water as tap water contains dissolved particles which may affect the results of an experiment. The correct **answer is (C).**

66. Enzymes speed up reactions by _____

A. utilizing ATP.

B. lowering pH, allowing reaction speed to increase.

C. increasing volume of substrate.

D. lowering energy of activation.

D. Lowering energy of activation.

Because enzymes are catalysts, they work the same way—they cause the formation of activated chemical complexes, which require a lower activation energy. Therefore, the **answer is (D).** ATP is an energy source for cells, and pH or volume changes may or may not affect reaction rate, so these answers can be eliminated.

67. When you step out of the shower, the floor feels colder on your feet than the bathmat. Which of the following is the correct explanation for this phenomenon?

   A. The floor is colder than the bathmat.

   B. Your feet have a chemical reaction with the floor, but not the bathmat.

   C. Heat is conducted more easily into the floor.

   D. Water is absorbed from your feet into the bathmat.

C. Heat is conducted more easily into the floor.

When you step out of the shower and onto a surface, the surface is most likely at room temperature, regardless of its composition (eliminating answer (A)). Your feet feel cold when heat is transferred from them to the surface, which happens more easily on a hard floor than a soft bathmat. This is because of differences in specific heat (the energy required to change temperature, which varies by material). Therefore, the **answer must be (C)**, i.e. heat is conducted more easily into the floor from your feet

68. Which of the following is *not* considered ethical behavior for a scientist?

   A. Using unpublished data and citing the source.

   B. Publishing data before other scientists have had a chance to replicate results.

   C. Collaborating with other scientists from different laboratories.

   D. Publishing work with an incomplete list of citations.

D. Publishing work with an incomplete list of citations.

One of the most important ethical principles for scientists is to cite all sources of data and analysis when publishing work. It is reasonable to use unpublished data (A), as long as the source is cited. Most science is published before other scientists replicate it (B), and frequently scientists collaborate with each other, in the same or different laboratories (C). These are all ethical choices. However, publishing work without the appropriate citations, is unethical. Therefore, the **answer is (D).**

69. The chemical equation for water formation is: $2H_2 + O_2 \rightarrow 2H_2O$. Which of the following is an *incorrect* interpretation of this equation?

  A. Two moles of hydrogen gas and one mole of oxygen gas combine to make two moles of water.

  B. Two grams of hydrogen gas and one gram of oxygen gas combine to make two grams of water.

  C. Two molecules of hydrogen gas and one molecule of oxygen gas combine to make two molecules of water.

  D. Four atoms of hydrogen (combined as a diatomic gas) and two atoms of oxygen (combined as a diatomic gas) combine to make two molecules of water.

B. Two grams of hydrogen gas and one gram of oxygen gas combine to make two grams of water.

In any chemical equation, the coefficients indicate the relative proportions of molecules (or atoms), or of moles of molecules. They do not refer to mass, because chemicals combine in repeatable combinations of molar ratio (i.e. number of moles), but vary in mass per mole of material. Therefore, the answer must be the only choice that does not refer to numbers of particles, i.e. **answer (B)**, which refers to grams, a unit of mass

70. **Energy is measured with the same units as** _____

  A. force.

  B. momentum.

  C. work.

  D. power.

C. Work.

In SI units, energy is measured in Joules, i.e. (mass)(length squared)/(time squared). This is the same unit as is used for work. You can verify this by calculating that since work is force times distance, the units work out to be the same. Force is measured in Newtons in SI; momentum is measured in (mass)(length)/(time); power is measured in Watts (which equal Joules/second). Therefore, the **answer must be (C)**.

71. **If the volume of a confined gas is increased, what happens to the pressure of the gas? You may assume that the gas behaves ideally, and that temperature and number of gas molecules remain constant.**

   A. The pressure increases.

   B. The pressure decreases.

   C. The pressure stays the same.

   D. There is not enough information given to answer this question.

B. The pressure decreases.

Because we are told that the gas behaves ideally, you may assume that it follows the Ideal Gas Law, i.e. PV = nRT. This means that an increase in volume must be associated with a decrease in pressure (i.e. higher T means lower P), because we are also given that all the components of the right side of the equation remain constant. Therefore, the **answer must be (B)**.

72. **A product of anaerobic respiration in animals is _____**

   A. carbon dioxide.

   B. lactic acid.

   C. oxygen.

   D. sodium chloride.

B. Lactic acid.

In animals, anaerobic respiration (i.e. respiration without the presence of oxygen) generates lactic acid as a byproduct. (Note that some anaerobic bacteria generate carbon dioxide from respiration of methane, and animals generate carbon dioxide in aerobic respiration.) Oxygen is not normally a by-product of respiration, though it is a product of photosynthesis, and sodium chloride is not strictly relevant in this question. Therefore, the **answer must be (B)**. By the way, lactic acid is believed to cause muscle soreness after anaerobic weight-lifting.

73. A Newton is fundamentally a measure of _____

    A. force.

    B. momentum.

    C. energy.

    D. gravity.

A. Force.

In SI units, force is measured in Newtons. Momentum and energy each have different units, without equivalent dimensions. A Newton is one (kilogram)(meter)/(second squared), while momentum is measured in (kilgram)(meter)/(second) and energy, in Joules, is (kilogram)(meter squared)/(second squared). Although "gravity" can be interpreted as the force of gravity, i.e. measured in Newtons, fundamentally it is not required. Therefore, the **answer is (A)**.

74. Which change does *not* affect enzyme rate?

    A. Increase the temperature.

    B. Add more substrate.

    C. Adjust the pH.

    D. Use a larger cell.

D. Use a larger cell.

Temperature, chemical amounts, and pH can all affect enzyme rate. However, the chemical reactions take place on a small enough scale that the overall cell size is not relevant. Therefore, the **answer is (D)**.

75. **Which of the following types of rock are made from magma?**

    A. Fossils.

    B. Sedimentary.

    C. Metamorphic.

    D. Igneous.

D. Igneous.

Few fossils are found in metamorphic rock and virtually none found in igneous rocks. Igneous rocks are formed from magma and magma is so hot that any organisms trapped by it are destroyed. Metamorphic rocks are formed by high temperatures and great pressures. When fluid sediments are transformed into solid sedimentary rocks, the process is known as lithification. The **answer is (D).**

76. **Which of the following is *not* an acceptable way for a student to acknowledge sources in a laboratory report?**

    A. The student tells his/her teacher what sources s/he used to write the report.

    B. The student uses footnotes in the text, with sources cited, but not in correct MLA format.

    C. The student uses endnotes in the text, with sources cited, in correct MLA format.

    D. The student attaches a separate bibliography, noting each use of sources.

A. The student tells his/her teacher what sources s/he used to write the report.

It may seem obvious, but students are often unaware that scientists need to cite all sources used. For the young adolescent, it is not always necessary to use official MLA format (though this should be taught at some point). Students may properly cite references in many ways, but these references must be in writing, with the original assignment. Therefore, the **answer is (A).**

77. **Animals with a notochord or a backbone are in the phylum**

    A. arthropoda.

    B. chordata.

    C. mollusca.

    D. mammalia.

B. Chordata.

The phylum arthropoda contains spiders and insects and phylum mollusca contain snails and squid. Mammalia is a class in the phylum chordata The **answer is (B).**

78. **Which of the following is a correct explanation for scientific 'evolution'?**

    A. Giraffes need to reach higher for leaves to eat, so their necks stretch. The giraffe babies are then born with longer necks. Eventually, there are more long-necked giraffes in the population.

    B. Giraffes with longer necks are able to reach more leaves, so they eat more and have more babies than other giraffes. Eventually, there are more long-necked giraffes in the population.

    C. Giraffes want to reach higher for leaves to eat, so they release enzymes into their bloodstream, which in turn causes fetal development of longer-necked giraffes. Eventually, there are more long-necked giraffes in the population.

    D. Giraffes with long necks are more attractive to other giraffes, so they get the best mating partners and have more babies. Eventually, there are more long-necked giraffes in the population.

B. Giraffes with longer necks are able to reach more leaves, so they eat more and have more babies than other giraffes. Eventually, there are more long-necked giraffes in the population.

Although evolution is often misunderstood, it occurs via natural selection. Organisms with a life/reproductive advantage will produce more offspring. Over many generations, this changes the proportions of the population. In any case, it is impossible for a stretched neck (A) or a fervent desire (C) to result in biologically mutated baby. Although there are traits that are naturally selected because of mate attractiveness and fitness (D), this is not the primary situation here, **so answer (B) is the best choice.**

79. Which of the following is a correct definition for 'chemical equilibrium'?

   A. Chemical equilibrium is when the forward and backward reaction rates are equal. The reaction may continue to proceed forward and backward.

   B. Chemical equilibrium is when the forward and backward reaction rates are equal, and equal to zero. The reaction does not continue.

   C. Chemical equilibrium is when there are equal quantities of reactants and products.

   D. Chemical equilibrium is when acids and bases neutralize each other fully.

A. Chemical equilibrium is when the forward and backward reaction rates are equal. The reaction may continue to proceed forward and backward.

Chemical equilibrium is defined as when the quantities of reactants and products are at a 'steady state' and no longer shifting, but the reaction may still proceed forward and backward. The rate of forward reaction must equal the rate of backward reaction. Note that there may or may not be equal amounts of chemicals, and that this is not restricted to a completed reaction or to an acid-base reaction. Therefore, the **answer is (A)**.

80. Which of the following data sets is properly represented by a bar graph?

   A. Number of people choosing to buy cars, vs. Color of car bought.

   B. Number of people choosing to buy cars, vs. Age of car customer.

   C. Number of people choosing to buy cars, vs. Distance from car lot to customer home.

   D. Number of people choosing to buy cars, vs. Time since last car purchase.

A. Number of people choosing to buy cars, vs. Color of car bought.

A bar graph should be used only for data sets in which the independent variable is non-continuous (discrete), e.g. gender, color, etc. Any continuous independent variable (age, distance, time, etc.) should yield a scatter-plot when the dependent variable is plotted. Therefore, the **answer must be (A)**.

81. In a science experiment, a student needs to dispense very small measured amounts of liquid into a well-mixed solution. Which of the following is the \ best choice for his/her equipment to use?

    A. Buret with Buret Stand, Stir-plate, Stirring Rod, Beaker.

    B. Buret with Buret Stand, Stir-plate, Beaker.

    C. Volumetric Flask, Dropper, Graduated Cylinder, Stirring Rod.

    D. Beaker, Graduated Cylinder, Stir-plate.

B. Buret with Buret Stand, Stir-plate, Beaker.

The most accurate and convenient way to dispense small measured amounts of liquid in the laboratory is with a buret, on a buret stand. To keep a solution well-mixed, a magnetic stir-plate is the most sensible choice, and the solution will usually be mixed in a beaker. Although other combinations of materials could be used for this experiment, **choice (B)** is thus the simplest and best.

82. A laboratory balance is most appropriately used to measure the mass of which of the following?

    A. Seven paper clips.

    B. Three oranges.

    C. Two hundred cells.

    D. One student's elbow.

A. Seven paper clips.

Usually, laboratory/classroom balances can measure masses between approximately 0.01 gram and 1 kilogram. Therefore, answer (B) is too heavy and answer (C) is too light. Answer (D) is silly, but it is a reminder to instruct students not to lean on the balances or put their things near them. **Answer (A)**, which is likely to have a mass of a few grams, is correct in this case.

83. All of the following are measured in units of length, *except* for:

    A. Perimeter.

    B. Distance.

    C. Radius.

    D. Area.

D. Area.

Perimeter is the distance around a shape; distance is equivalent to length; radius is the distance from the center (e.g. in a circle) to the edge. Area, however, is the squared-length-units measure of the size of a two-dimensional surface. Therefore, **the answer is (D)**.

84. What is specific gravity?

    A. The mass of an object.

    B. The ratio of the density of a substance to the density of water.

    C. Density.

    D. The pull of the earth's gravity on an object.

B. The ratio of the density of a substance to the density of water.

Mass is a measure of the amount of matter in an object. Density is the mass of a substance contained per unit of volume. Weight is the measure of the earth's pull of gravity on an object. The only option here is the ratio of the density of a substance to the density of water, **answer (B).**

85. What is the most accurate description of the Water Cycle?

A. Rain comes from clouds, filling the ocean. The water then evaporates and becomes clouds again.

B. Water circulates from rivers into groundwater and back, while water vapor circulates in the atmosphere.

C. Water is conserved except for chemical or nuclear reactions, and any drop of water could circulate through clouds, rain, ground-water, and surface-water.

D. Weather systems cause chemical reactions to break water into its atoms.

C. Water is conserved except for chemical or nuclear reactions, and any drop of water could circulate through clouds, rain, ground-water, and surface-water.

All natural chemical cycles, including the Water Cycle, depend on the principle of Conservation of Mass. (For water, unlike for elements such as Nitrogen, chemical reactions may cause sources or sinks of water molecules.) Any drop of water may circulate through the hydrologic system, ending up in a cloud, as rain, or as surface- or ground-water. Although answers (A) and (B) describe parts of the water cycle, the most comprehensive and correct **answer is (C)**.

86. The scientific name *Canis familiaris* refers to the animal's _____

A. kingdom and phylum.

B. genus and species.

C. class and species.

D. type and family.

B. Genus and species.

To answer this question, you must be aware that genus and species are the most specific way to identify an organism, and that usually the genus is capitalized and the species, immediately following, is not. Furthermore, it helps to recall that 'Canis' is the genus for dogs, or canines. Therefore, the **answer must be (B)**. If you did not remember these details, you might recall that there is no such kingdom as 'Canis,' and that there isn't a category 'type' in official taxonomy. This could eliminate answers (A) and (D).

87. Members of the same animal species _____

    A. look identical.

    B. never adapt differently.

    C. are able to reproduce with one another.

    D. are found in the same location.

C. Are able to reproduce with one another.

Although members of the same animal species may look alike (A), adapt alike (B), or be found near one another (D), the only requirement is that they be able to reproduce with one another. This ability to reproduce within the group is considered the hallmark of a species. Therefore, the **answer is (C)**.

88. Which of the following is/are true about scientists?

    I.   Scientists usually work alone.
    II.   Scientists usually work with other scientists.
    III.   Scientists achieve more prestige from new discoveries than from replicating established results.
    IV.   Scientists keep records of their own work, but do not publish it for outside review.

    A. I and IV only.

    B. II only.

    C. II and III only.

    D. III and IV only.

C. II and III only.

In the scientific community, scientists nearly always work in teams, both within their institutions and across several institutions. This eliminates (I) and requires (II), leaving only **answer choices (B) and (C)**. Scientists do achieve greater prestige from new discoveries, so the answer must be (C). Note that scientists must publish their work in peer-reviewed journals, eliminating (IV) in any case.

89. **What is necessary for ion diffusion to occur spontaneously?**

    A. Carrier proteins.

    B. Energy from an outside source.

    C. A concentration gradient.

    D. Cell flagellae.

C. A concentration gradient.

Spontaneous diffusion occurs when random motion leads particles to increase entropy by equalizing concentrations. Particles tend to move into places of lower concentration. Therefore, a concentration gradient is required, and the **answer is (C)**. No proteins (A), outside energy (B), or flagellae (D) are required for this process.

90. **All of the following are considered Newton's Laws *except* for:**

    A. An object in motion will continue in motion unless acted upon by an outside force.

    B. For every action force, there is an equal and opposite reaction force.

    C. Nature abhors a vacuum.

    D. Mass can be considered the ratio of force to acceleration.

C. Nature abhors a vacuum.

Newton's Laws include his law of inertia (an object in motion (or at rest) will stay in motion (or at rest) until acted upon by an outside force) (A), his law that (Force)=(Mass)(Acceleration) (D), and his equal and opposite reaction force law (B). Therefore, the **answer to this question is (C)**, because "Nature abhors a vacuum" is not one of these.

91. **A cup of hot liquid and a cup of cold liquid are both sitting in a room at comfortable room temperature and humidity. Both cups are thin plastic. Which of the following is a true statement?**

   A. There will be fog on the outside of the hot liquid cup, and also fog on the outside of the cold liquid cup.

   B. There will be fog on the outside of the hot liquid cup, but not on the cold liquid cup.

   C. There will be fog on the outside of the cold liquid cup, but not on the hot liquid cup.

   D. There will not be fog on the outside of either cup.

C. **There will be fog on the outside of the cold liquid cup, but not on the hot liquid cup.**

Fog forms on the outside of a cup when the contents of the cup are colder than the surrounding air, and the cup material is not a perfect insulator. This happens because the air surrounding the cup is cooled to a lower temperature than the ambient room, so it has a lower saturation point for water vapor. Although the humidity had been reasonable in the warmer air, when that air circulates near the colder region and cools, water condenses onto the cup's outside surface. This phenomenon is also visible when someone takes a hot shower, and the mirror gets foggy. The mirror surface is cooler than the ambient air, and provides a surface for water condensation. Furthermore, the same phenomenon is why defrosters on car windows send heat to the windows—the warmer window does not permit as much condensation. Therefore, the correct **answer is (C)**.

92. A ball rolls down a smooth hill. You may ignore air resistance. Which of the following is a true statement?

A. The ball has more energy at the start of its descent than just before it hits the bottom of the hill, because it is higher up at the beginning.

B. The ball has less energy at the start of its descent than just before it hits the bottom of the hill, because it is moving more quickly at the end.

C. The ball has the same energy throughout its descent, because positional energy is converted to energy of motion.

D. The ball has the same energy throughout its descent, because a single object (such as a ball) cannot gain or lose energy.

C. The ball has the same energy throughout its descent, because positional energy is converted to energy of motion.

The principle of Conservation of Energy states that (except in cases of nuclear reaction, when energy may be created or destroyed by conversion to mass), "Energy is neither created nor destroyed, but may be transformed." Answers (A) and (B) give you a hint in this question—it is true that the ball has more Potential Energy when it is higher, and that it has more Kinetic Energy when it is moving quickly at the bottom of its descent. However, the total sum of all kinds of energy in the ball remains constant, if we neglect 'losses' to heat/friction. Note that a single object can and does gain or lose energy when the energy is transferred to or from a different object. Conservation of Energy applies to systems, not to individual objects unless they are isolated. Therefore, the **answer must be (C)**.

93. **A long silver bar has a temperature of 50 degrees Celsius at one end and 0 degrees Celsius at the other end. The bar will reach thermal equilibrium (barring outside influence) by the process of heat _____**

    A. conduction.

    B. convection.

    C. radiation.

    D. phase change.

A. conduction.

Heat conduction is the process of heat transfer via solid contact. The molecules in a warmer region vibrate more rapidly, jostling neighboring molecules and accelerating them. This is the dominant heat transfer process in a solid with no outside influences. Recall, also, that convection is heat transfer by way of fluid currents; radiation is heat transfer via electromagnetic waves; phase change can account for heat transfer in the form of shifts in matter phase. The answer to this question must **therefore be (A).**

94. _____ **are cracks in the plates of the earth's crust, along which the plates move.**

    A. Faults

    B. Ridges

    C. Earthquakes

    D. Volcanoes

A. Faults.

Faults are cracks in the earth's crust, and when the earth moves, that is called an earthquake. Faults may lead to mismatched edges of ground, forming ridges, and ground shape may also be determined by volcanoes. The answer to this question must **therefore be (A).**

95. **Fossils are usually found in _____ rock.**

    A. igneous.

    B. sedimentary.

    C. metamorphic.

    D. cumulus.

B. Sedimentary

Fossils are formed by layers of dirt and sand settling around organisms, hardening, and taking an imprint of the organisms. When the organism decays, the hardened imprint is left behind. This is most likely to happen in rocks that form from layers of settling dirt and sand, i.e. sedimentary rock. Note that igneous rock is formed from molten rock from volcanoes (lava), while metamorphic rock can be formed from any rock under very high temperature and pressure changes. 'Cumulus' is a descriptor for clouds, not rocks. The best answer is **therefore (B)**.

96. **Which of the following is *not* a common type of acid in 'acid rain' or acidified surface water?**

    A. Nitric acid.

    B. Sulfuric acid.

    C. Carbonic acid.

    D. Hydrofluoric acid.

D. Hydrofluoric acid.

Acid rain forms predominantly from pollutant oxides in the air (usually nitrogen-based NO_x or sulfur-based SO_x), which become hydrated into their acids (nitric or sulfuric acid). Because of increased levels of carbon dioxide pollution, carbonic acid is also common in acidified surface water environments. Hydrofluoric acid can be found, but it is much less common. In general, carbon, nitrogen, and sulfur are much more prevalent in the environment than fluorine. Therefore, the **answer is (D)**.

97. Which of the following is *not* true about phase change in matter?

  A. Solid water and liquid ice can coexist at water's freezing point.

  B. At 7 degrees Celsius, water is always in liquid phase.

  C. Matter changes phase when enough energy is gained or lost.

  D. Different phases of matter are characterized by differences in molecular motion.

B. At 7 degrees Celsius, water is always in liquid phase.

According to the molecular theory of matter, molecular motion determines the 'phase' of the matter, and the energy in the matter determines the speed of molecular motion. Solids have vibrating molecules that are in fixed relative positions; liquids have faster molecular motion than their solid forms, and the molecules may move more freely but must still be in contact with one another; gases have even more energy and more molecular motion. (Other phases, such as plasma, are yet more energetic.) At the 'freezing point' or 'boiling point' of a substance, both relevant phases may be present. For instance, water at zero degrees Celsius may be composed of some liquid and some solid, or all liquid, or all solid. Pressure changes, in addition to temperature changes, can cause phase changes. For example, nitrogen can be liquefied under high pressure, even though its boiling temperature is very low. Therefore, the **correct answer must be (B)**. Water may be a liquid at that temperature, but it may also be a solid, depending on ambient pressure.

98. Which of the following is the longest (largest) unit of geological time?

  A. Solar Year.

  B. Epoch.

  C. Period.

  D. Era.

D. Era.

Geological time is measured by many units, but the longest unit listed here (and indeed the longest used to describe the biological development of the planet) is the Era. Eras are subdivided into Periods, which are further divided into Epochs. Therefore, the **answer is (D)**.

99. **Extensive use of antibacterial soap has been found to increase the virulence of certain infections in hospitals. Which of the following might be an \ explanation for this phenomenon?**

    A. Antibacterial soaps do not kill viruses.

    B. Antibacterial soaps do not incorporate the same antibiotics used as medicine.

    C. Antibacterial soaps kill a lot of bacteria, and only the hardiest ones survive to reproduce.

    D. Antibacterial soaps can be very drying to the skin.

C. Antibacterial soaps kill a lot of bacteria, and only the hardiest ones survive to reproduce.

All of the answer choices in this question are true statements, but the question specifically asks for a cause of increased disease virulence in hospitals. This phenomenon is due to natural selection: the bacteria that can survive contact with antibacterial soap are the strongest ones, and without other bacteria competing for resources, they have more opportunity to flourish. This problem has led to several antibiotic-resistant bacterial diseases in hospitals nation-wide. Therefore, the **answer is (C)**. However, note that answers (A) and (D) may be additional problems with over-reliance on antibacterial products.

100. **Which of the following is a correct explanation for astronaut 'weightlessness'?**

    A. Astronauts continue to feel the pull of gravity in space, but they are so far from planets that the force is small.

    B. Astronauts continue to feel the pull of gravity in space, but spacecraft have such powerful engines that those forces dominate, reducing effective weight.

    C. Astronauts do not feel the pull of gravity in space, because space is a vacuum.

    D. Astronauts do not feel the pull of gravity in space, because black hole forces dominate the force field, reducing their masses.

A. Astronauts continue to feel the pull of gravity in space, but they are so far from planets that the force is small.

Gravity acts over tremendous distances in space (theoretically, infinite distance, though certainly at least as far as any astronaut has traveled). However, gravitational force is inversely proportional to distance squared from a massive body. This means that when an astronaut is in space, s/he is far enough from the center of mass of any planet that the gravitational force is very small, and s/he feels 'weightless'. Space is mostly empty (i.e. vacuum), and there are some black holes, and spacecraft do have powerful engines. However, none of these has the effect attributed to it in the incorrect answer choices (B), (C), or (D). The answer to this question must **therefore be (A).**

101. **The theory of 'sea floor spreading' explains _____**

    A. the shapes of the continents.

    B. how continents collide.

    C. how continents move apart.

    D. how continents sink to become part of the ocean floor.

C. How continents move apart.

In the theory of 'sea floor spreading', the movement of the ocean floor causes continents to spread apart from one another. This occurs because crust plates split apart, and new material is added to the plate edges. This process pulls the continents apart, or may create new separations, and is believed to have caused the formation of the Atlantic Ocean. Therefore, the **answer is (C).**

102. **Which of the following animals are most likely to live in a tropical rain forest?**

    A. Reindeer.

    B. Monkeys.

    C. Puffins.

    D. Bears.

B. Monkeys.

The tropical rain forest biome is hot and humid, and is very fertile—it is thought to contain almost half of the world's species. Reindeer (A), puffins (C), and bears (D), however, are usually found in much colder climates. There are several species of monkeys that thrive in hot, humid climates, so **answer (B) is correct.**

103. **Which of the following is *not* a type of volcano?**

    A. Shield Volcanoes.

    B. Composite Volcanoes.

    C. Stratus Volcanoes.

    D. Cinder Cone Volcanoes.

C. Stratus Volcanoes.

There are three types of volcanoes. Shield volcanoes (A) are associated with non-violent eruptions and repeated lava flow over time. Composite volcanoes (B) are built from both lava flow and layers of ash and cinders. Cinder cone volcanoes (D) are associated with violent eruptions, such that lava is thrown into the air and becomes ash or cinder before falling and accumulating. **'Stratus' (C)** is a type of cloud, not volcano, so it is the correct answer to this question.

104. Which of the following is *not* a property of metalloids?

    A. Metalloids are solids at standard temperature and pressure.

    B. Metalloids can conduct electricity to a limited extent.

    C. Metalloids are found in groups 13 through 17.

    D. Metalloids all favor ionic bonding.

D. Metalloids all favor ionic bonding.

Metalloids are substances that have characteristics of both metals and nonmetals, including limited conduction of electricity and solid phase at standard temperature and pressure. Metalloids are found in a 'stair-step' pattern from Boron in group 13 through Astatine in group 17. Some metalloids, e.g. Silicon, favor covalent bonding. Others, e.g. Astatine, can bond ionically. Therefore, **the answer is (D).** Recall that metals/nonmetals/metalloids are not strictly defined by Periodic Table group, so their bonding is unlikely to be consistent with one another.

105. Which of these is a true statement about loamy soil?

    A. Loamy soil is gritty and porous.

    B. Loamy soil is smooth and a good barrier to water.

    C. Loamy soil is hostile to microorganisms.

    D. Loamy soil is velvety and clumpy.

D. Loamy soil is velvety and clumpy.

The three classes of soil by texture are: Sandy (gritty and porous), Clay (smooth, greasy, and most impervious to water), and Loamy (velvety, clumpy, and able to hold water and let water flow through). In addition, loamy soils are often the most fertile soils. Therefore, the **answer must be (D)**.

106. Lithification refers to the process by which unconsolidated sediments are transformed into _____

    A. metamorphic rocks.

    B. sedimentary rocks.

    C. igneous rocks.

    D. lithium oxide.

B. Sedimentary rocks.

Lithification is the process of sediments coming together to form rocks, i.e. sedimentary rock formation. Metamorphic and igneous rocks are formed via other processes (heat and pressure or volcano, respectively). Lithium oxide shares a word root with 'lithification' but is otherwise unrelated to this question. Therefore, the **answer must be (B)**.

107. Igneous rocks can be classified according to which of the following?

    A. Texture.

    B. Composition.

    C. Formation process.

    D. All of the above.

D. All of the above.

Igneous rocks, which form from the crystallization of molten lava, are classified according to many of their characteristics, including texture, composition, and how they were formed. Therefore, **the answer is (D)**.

108. Which of the following is the most accurate definition of a nonrenewable resource?

    A. A nonrenewable resource is never replaced once used.

    B. A nonrenewable resource is replaced on a timescale that is very long relative to human life-spans.

    C. A nonrenewable resource is a resource that can only be manufactured by humans.

    D. A nonrenewable resource is a species that has already become extinct.

B. A nonrenewable resource is replaced on a timescale that is very long relative to human life- spans.

Renewable resources are those that are renewed, or replaced, in time for humans to use more of them. Examples include fast-growing plants, animals, or oxygen gas. (Note that while sunlight is often considered a renewable resource, it is actually a nonrenewable but extremely abundant resource.) Nonrenewable resources are those that renew themselves only on very long timescales, usually geologic timescales. Examples include minerals, metals, or fossil fuels. Therefore, the **correct answer is (B)**.

109. The theory of 'continental drift' is supported by which of the following?

    A. The way the shapes of South America and Europe fit together.

    B. The way the shapes of Europe and Asia fit together.

    C. The way the shapes of South America and Africa fit together.

    D. The way the shapes of North America and Antarctica fit together.

C. The way the shapes of South America and Africa fit together.

The theory of 'continental drift' states that many years ago, there was one land mass on the earth ('pangea'). This land mass broke apart via earth crust motion, and the continents drifted apart as separate pieces. This is supported by the shapes of South America and Africa, which seem to fit together like puzzle pieces if you look at a globe. Note that answer choices (A), (B), and (D) give either land masses that do not fit together, or those that are still attached to each other. Therefore, the **answer must be (C)**.

110. When water falls to a cave floor and evaporates, it may deposit calcium carbonate. This process leads to the formation of which of the following?

A. Stalactites.

B. Stalagmites.

C. Fault lines.

D. Sedimentary rocks.

B. Stalagmites.

To answer this question, recall the trick to remember the kinds of crystals formed in caves. Stalactites have a 'T' in them, because they form hanging from the ceiling (resembling a 'T'). Stalagmites have an 'M' in them, because they make bumps on the floor (resembling an 'M'). Note that fault lines and sedimentary rocks are irrelevant to this question. Therefore, **the answer must be (B)**.

111. A child has type O blood. Her father has type A blood, and her mother has type B blood. What are the genotypes of the father and mother, respectively?

A. AO and BO.

B. AA and AB.

C. OO and BO.

D. AO and BB.

A. AO and BO.

Because O blood is recessive, the child must have inherited two O's—one from each of her parents. Since her father has type A blood, his genotype must be AO; likewise her mother's blood must be BO. Therefore, only **answer (A)** can be correct.

112. Which of the following is the best definition for 'meteorite'?

A. A meteorite is a mineral composed of mica and feldspar.

B. A meteorite is material from outer space, that has struck the earth's surface.

C. A meteorite is an element that has properties of both metals and nonmetals.

D. A meteorite is a very small unit of length measurement.

B. A meteorite is material from outer space, that has struck the earth's surface.

Meteoroids are pieces of matter in space, composed of particles of rock and metal. If a meteoroid travels through the earth's atmosphere, friction causes burning and a "shooting star"—i.e. a meteor. If the meteor strikes the earth's surface, it is known as a meterorite. Note that although the suffix –ite often means a mineral, answer (A) is incorrect. Answer (C) refers to a 'metalloid' rather than a 'meteorite', and answer (D) is simply a misleading pun on 'meter'. Therefore, the **answer is (B)**.

113. A white flower is crossed with a red flower. Which of the following is a sign of incomplete dominance?

A. Pink flowers.

B. Red flowers.

C. White flowers.

D. No flowers.

A. Pink flowers.

Incomplete dominance means that neither the red nor the white gene is strong enough to suppress the other. Therefore both are expressed, leading in this case to the formation of pink flowers. Therefore, the **answer is (A)**.

114. What is the source for most of the United States' drinking water?

    A. Desalinated ocean water.

    B. Surface water (lakes, streams, mountain runoff).

    C. Rainfall into municipal reservoirs.

    D. Groundwater.

D. Groundwater.

Groundwater currently provides drinking water for 53% of the population of the United States. (Although groundwater is often less polluted than surface water, it can be contaminated and it is very hard to clean once it is polluted. If too much groundwater is used from one area, then the ground may sink or shift, or local salt water may intrude from ocean boundaries.) The other answer choices can be used for drinking water, but they are not the most widely used. Therefore, **the answer is (D)**.

115. Which is the correct sequence of insect development?

    A. Egg, pupa, larva, adult.

    B. Egg, larva, pupa, adult.

    C. Egg, adult, larva, pupa.

    D. Pupa, egg, larva, adult.

B. Egg, larva, pupa, adult.

An insect begins as an egg, hatches into a larva (e.g. caterpillar), forms a pupa (e.g. cocoon), and emerges as an adult (e.g. moth). Therefore, the **answer is (B)**.

116. **A wrasse (fish) cleans the teeth of other fish by eating away plaque. This is an example of _____ between the fish.**

    A. parasitism.

    B. symbiosis (mutualism).

    C. competition.

    D. predation.

B. Symbiosis (mutualism).

When both species benefit from their interaction in their habitat, this is called 'symbiosis', or 'mutualism'. In this example, the wrasse benefits from having a source of food, and the other fish benefit by having healthier teeth. Note that 'parasitism' is when one species benefits at the expense of the other, 'competition' is when two species compete with one another for the same habitat or food, and 'predation' is when one species feeds on another. Therefore, the **answer is (B)**.

117. **What is the main obstacle to using nuclear fusion for obtaining electricity?**

    A. Nuclear fusion produces much more pollution than nuclear fission.

    B. There is no obstacle; most power plants us nuclear fusion today.

    C. Nuclear fusion requires very high temperature and activation energy.

    D. The fuel for nuclear fusion is extremely expensive.

C. Nuclear fusion requires very high temperature and activation energy.

Nuclear fission is the usual process for power generation in nuclear power plants. This is carried out by splitting nuclei to release energy. The sun's energy is generated by nuclear fusion, i.e. combination of smaller nuclei into a larger nucleus. Fusion creates much less radioactive waste, but it requires extremely high temperature and activation energy, so it is not yet feasible for electricity generation. Therefore, the **answer is (C)**.

118. Which of the following is a true statement about radiation exposure and air travel?

    A. Air travel exposes humans to radiation, but the level is not significant for most people.

    B. Air travel exposes humans to so much radiation that it is recommended as a method of cancer treatment.

    C. Air travel does not expose humans to radiation.

    D. Air travel may or may not expose humans to radiation, but it has not yet been determined.

A. Air travel exposes humans to radiation, but the level is not significant for most people.

Humans are exposed to background radiation from the ground and in the atmosphere, but these levels are not considered hazardous under most circumstances, and these levels have been studied extensively. Air travel does create more exposure to atmospheric radiation, though this is much less than people usually experience through dental X-rays or other medical treatment. People whose jobs or lifestyles include a great deal of air flight may be at increased risk for certain cancers from excessive radiation exposure. Therefore, the **answer is (A)**.

119. Which process(es) result(s) in a haploid chromosome number?

    A. Mitosis.

    B. Meiosis.

    C. Both mitosis and meiosis.

    D. Neither mitosis nor meiosis.

B. Meiosis.

Meiosis is the division of sex cells. The resulting chromosome number is half the number of parent cells, i.e. a 'haploid chromosome number'. Mitosis, however, is the division of other cells, in which the chromosome number is the same as the parent cell chromosome number. Therefore, the **answer is (B)**.

120. Which of the following is *not* a member of Kingdom Fungi?

    A. Mold.

    B. Blue-green algae.

    C. Mildew.

    D. Mushrooms.

B. Algae.

Mold (A), mildew (C), and mushrooms (D) are all types of fungus. Blue-green algae, however, is in Kingdom Monera. Therefore, the **answer is (B)**.

121. Which of the following organisms use spores to reproduce?

    A. Fish.

    B. Flowering plants.

    C. Conifers.

    D. Ferns.

D. Ferns.

Ferns, in Division Pterophyta, reproduce with spores and flagellated sperm. Flowering plants reproduce via seeds, and conifers reproduce via seeds protected in cones (e.g. pinecone). Fish, of course, reproduce sexually. Therefore, the **answer is (D)**.

122. What is the main difference between the 'condensation hypothesis' and the 'tidal hypothesis' for the origin of the solar system?

A. The tidal hypothesis can be tested, but the condensation hypothesis cannot.

B. The tidal hypothesis proposes a near collision of two stars pulling on each other, but the condensation hypothesis proposes condensation of rotating clouds of dust and gas.

C. The tidal hypothesis explains how tides began on planets such as Earth, but the condensation hypothesis explains how water vapor became liquid on Earth.

D. The tidal hypothesis is based on Aristotelian physics, but the condensation hypothesis is based on Newtonian mechanics.

B. The tidal hypothesis proposes a near collision of two stars pulling on each other, but the condensation hypothesis proposes condensation of rotating clouds of dust and gas.

Most scientists believe the 'condensation hypothesis,' i.e. that the solar system began when rotating clouds of dust and gas condensed into the sun and planets. A minority opinion is the 'tidal hypothesis,' i.e. that the sun almost collided with a large star. The large star's gravitational field would have then pulled gases out of the sun; these gases are thought to have begun to orbit the sun and condense into planets. Because both of these hypotheses deal with ancient, unrepeatable events, neither can be tested, eliminating answer (A). Note that both 'tidal' and 'condensation' have additional meanings in physics, but those are not relevant here, eliminating answer (C). Both hypotheses are based on best guesses using modern physics, eliminating answer (D). Therefore, the **answer is (B)**.

123. Which of the following units is *not* a measure of distance?

A. AU (astronomical unit).

B. Light year.

C. Parsec.

D. Lunar year.

D. Lunar year.

Although the terminology is sometimes confusing, it is important to remember that a 'light year' (B) refers to the distance that light can travel in a year. Astronomical Units (AU) (A) also measure distance, and one AU is the distance between the sun and the earth. Parsecs (C) also measure distance, and are used in astronomical measurement—they are very large, and are usually used to measure interstellar distances. A lunar year, or any other kind of year for a planet or moon, is the *time* measure of that body's orbit. Therefore, the answer to this **question is (D).**

124. The salinity of ocean water is closest to _____.

A. 0.035 %

B. 0.35 %

C. 3.5 %

D. 35 %

C. 3.5 %

Salinity, or concentration of dissolved salt, can be measured in mass ratio (i.e. mass of salt divided by mass of sea water). For Earth's oceans, the salinity is approximately 3.5 %, or 35 parts per thousand. Note that answers (A) and (D) can be eliminated, because (A) is so dilute as to be hardly saline, while (D) is so concentrated that it would not support ocean life. Therefore, the **answer is (C).**

125. Which of the following will not change in a chemical reaction?

    A. Number of moles of products.

    B. Atomic number of one of the reactants.

    C. Mass (in grams) of one of the reactants.

    D. Rate of reaction.

B. Atomic number of one of the reactants.

Atomic number, i.e. the number of protons in a given element, is constant unless involved in a nuclear reaction. Meanwhile, the amounts (measured in moles (A) or in grams(C)) of reactants and products change over the course of a chemical reaction, and the rate of a chemical reaction (D) may change due to internal or external processes. Therefore, the **answer is (B)**.

Printed in the United States
57350LVS00006B/35

9 781581 971088